EANE VALLEY HIGH SCHOOL
JACKSON ROAD
CONGLETON
CHESHIRE CW12 1NT

BARRY HINES
TWO MEN FROM DERBY
and
SHOOTING STARS

Introduction, notes and activities
by Peter Shepherd

Heinemann Educational Publishers
Halley Court, Jordan Hill, Oxford OX2 8EJ
a division of Reed Educational & Professional Publishing Ltd
MELBOURNE   AUCKLAND
FLORENCE   PRAGUE   MADRID   ATHENS
SINGAPORE   TOKYO   SAO PAULO
CHICAGO   PORTSMOUTH (NH)   MEXICO
IBADAN   GABORONE   JOHANNESBURG
KAMPALA   NAIROBI

Two Men from Derby
Copyright © 1976 Barry Hines

Shooting Stars
Copyright © 1993 Barry Hines/Granada Television Ltd

Introduction, notes and activities © 1993 Peter Shepherd

Published in the *Heinemann Plays* series 1993

97 98 99 2000 10 9 8 7 6 5 4 3 2

A catalogue record for this book is available from the British Library on request.

ISBN 0 435 23298 3

All rights whatsoever in these plays are strictly reserved and application for performance, etc. should be made before rehearsal to Lemon, Unna and Durbridge Ltd, 24 Pottery Lane, Holland Park, London W11 4LZ. No performance may be given unless a licence has been obtained.

Cover design by Keith Pointing

Original design by Jeffery White Creative Associates

Typeset by Taurus Graphics, Kidlington, Oxon

Printed by Clays Ltd, St Ives plc

CONTENTS

Introduction	v
Two Men from Derby	1
List of Characters	2
The Play	3
Shooting Stars	29
List of Characters	30
The Play	31

Questions and Explorations

Two Men from Derby
1	Keeping Track	106
2	Explorations: A Characters	107
	B Themes	108
	C Drama	110
	D Further activities	111
	Glossary	112

Shooting Stars
1	Keeping Track	113
2	Explorations: A Characters	115
	B Themes	116
	C Drama	118
	D Further activities	119
	Glossary	120

INTRODUCTION

Sugden placed the ball on the centre spot and looked round at his team. There was only Billy out of position. He was standing between the full backs, the three of them forming a domino pattern with the half backs. The goal was empty. Mr Sugden pointed at it.

'There's no one in goal!'

His team looked round to confirm this observation, but Tibbut's team had beaten them to it just by looking straight ahead.

'Casper! What position are you supposed to be playing?'

Billy looked to the Right Back; the Left Back, the Right Back again. Neither of them supplied the answer so he answered the question himself.

'I don't know, Sir. Inside Right?'

This answer made 1: Mr Sugden angry, 2: the boys laugh.

'Don't talk ridiculous, lad! How can you be playing Inside Right back there?'

He looked up at the sky.

'God help us; fifteen years old and still doesn't know the positions of a football team!'

So begins the famous comic football match in Barry Hines' most popular novel *A Kestrel for a Knave*, the story of the luckless Billy Casper struggling for respect and breaking the rules of football, school and life in general. The interaction between the boys and the domineering PE teacher Mr Sugden as the game progresses is both funny and serious. The central struggle between Billy's wish to end the game and get home to his kestrel hawk and Sugden's determination to win at any cost is a delicate balance.

Football is the backdrop of many of Barry Hines' novels, plays and screenplays. In the plays in this volume, football is central to the plot. However, neither is about football, any more than *A Kestrel for a Knave* is. What they do have in common is that the central characters in both have the desire and opportunity to escape from poverty and oppression.

Shooting Stars is a fast-moving, hard-hitting television play first broadcast in 1990. It is the story of Gary and his friends who kidnap the star striker of City Football Club.

On first appearances, Calvin Clark seems to be the opposite of Gary. The footballer has everything – expensive clothes, the pick of the girls, an exciting job, a luxurious flat, an expensive car, opportunities and a future . . . and Gary has nothing. Gradually we discover that their lives have some surprising similarities and Gary is able to teach Calvin some lessons. Gary is not unlike Billy Casper: both in search of respect, and both take quite different risks to achieve it.

In the screenplay, football is a glamorous and risky business. Just as *A Kestrel for a Knave* is about education not falconry, *Shooting Stars* is not about football but about ambition, respect and success.

Two Men from Derby is set in a miner's home near Sheffield in 1930. Two football talent scouts from Derby County come to see the husband, Dick, to ask him to come for a trial for the club. But Dick, despite having agreed the date and time of this meeting, never materialises. His wife, Freda, who is the central character in the play, initiates a desperate search party for him around the district, but with no success.

As with *Shooting Stars* the play is not about football itself but about the opportunity it offers for escape from poverty and drudgery. For Dick and Freda's lives are grindingly hard, especially Freda's. Six months' pregnant, she carries on heavy and constant domestic work while talking to the two scouts. As the play wears on, it becomes clear that, although married only seven months, she already dreads the life ahead of her – a constant stream of children and back-breakingly hard work, like the life her own mother led.

For Freda, the prospect of a highly-paid job and well-equipped house for Dick as a footballer promises release. The £15 a week he would be paid by Derby County is equivalent to about £420 today. By comparison his miner's wages amount to the equivalent of £84 to £112 a week. In addition, footballing is a far safer job than mining – Freda, like many miners' wives, lives in dread of pit accidents.

Dick, however, is clearly not willing to put himself to the test in the trial, and risk losing his status in the community by failing. Although Dick's job is hard and dangerous, it is clear in the play that he has many pursuits outside it and a lot of freedom in his spare time. Despite the lowness of his wages, he only hands part of them over to Freda to run the house and has the rest to spend on himself. He has much more to lose than she in risking the football trials and life in Derby.

Barry Hines wrote both plays with an insider's understanding having worked in both mining and football. He was born in the mining village of Hoyland Common, near Barnsley in 1939. He was educated at Ecclesfield Grammar School, where he was selected for the England Grammar Schools' football team. On leaving school, he worked as an Apprentice Mining Surveyor and played football for Barnsley, before entering Loughborough Training College to study Physical Education. He taught for several years in London and South Yorkshire before becoming a full-time novelist and playwright.

His novels include: *The Blinder, A Kestrel for a Knave, First Signs, The Gamekeeper, The Price of Coal, Looks and Smiles* and *Unfinished Business*. Cinema, radio and television credits include *Kes, Looks and Smiles* (Prix du Cinéma Contemporain, Cannes 1981), *Billy's Last Stand, Speech Day, Two Men from Derby, The Price of Coal, The Gamekeeper, A Question of Leadership, Threads, Shooting Stars* and *Born Kicking*.

He writes of his work:

'My novels are mostly about working-class life. They are about people who live on council estates or in small terraced houses. The men work in mines and steelworks, the women in underpaid menial jobs – or, increasingly, are on the dole. I feel a strong sense of social injustice on behalf of these people which stems from my own mining background. The hardness and danger of that life (my grandfather was killed down the pit, my father was injured several times) formed my attitudes and made me a socialist.

My political viewpoint is the mainspring of my work. It fuels my energy, which is fine, as long as the characters remain believable and do not degenerate into dummies merely mouthing my own beliefs. However, I would rather risk being didactic than lapsing into blandness – or end up writing novels about writers writing novels. If that happens it will be time to hang up the biro.'

At the end of the play text, you will find ideas for follow-up work. The first section, *Keeping Track*, can be followed scene by scene as you read the play and contains questions to help you think clearly about the action in each scene. The second section, *Explorations*, has extended activities to help you think more broadly about the characters, themes and issues in the play as a whole.

Two Men from Derby

Barry Hines

LIST OF CHARACTERS

Freda
George Hirst
Joe Kenny
Winnie
Stanley

TWO MEN FROM DERBY

The play is set in 1930 in the kitchen of a terraced house in a mining village in the North of England. It is washday. In order to accommodate the washing tackle in the small room, Freda has had to move the furniture around to make the space on the hearth bigger. She has pushed the table back against the dresser and rolled the hearth rug back.

The room is crowded and untidy and there are separate piles of clothes on the floor and on the table. The kitchen is hot and steamy. This is the equipment Freda is using for washing: two peggy tubs, a peggy legs, a rubbing board and a mangle. There is also a boiler working. This is set between the fireplace and the sink in the corner. As well as doing her washing, Freda is also preparing her husband's dinner, and she also has a pancheon of dough rising in the hearth.

She is extremely busy and it is important that Freda is seen to be working hard throughout the play. Her activity should contrast with the inactivity of the two men who come to visit the house. It would be inconceivable for them to help her with one of the heavy jobs, for example, mending the fire, or emptying a tub, even though they can see that she is pregnant. The nature of her work is taken for granted by them. The play opens with Freda washing the sheets in one of the tubs. She soaps them and rubs them up and down the rubbing board. Then she puts them through the mangle and places them in a pile on the table. She then puts the towels to soak in this tub. The whites (shirts, underwear, handkerchiefs, pillow slips) are now ready to come out of the boiler.

Freda fishes them out with a stick, places them in a bowl so that they do not drip all over the floor, and transfers them to the second tub which contains cold rinsing water. Using a ladling can, Freda now tops up the boiler with cold water from the tap and puts the sheets in to boil. Freda now starts to peggy the whites in the rinsing tub with the peggy legs. She then takes them out, mangles them and places the damp clothes in a pile on the table. While she is doing this there is a knock on the door.

Freda   Wait a minute!

She finishes mangling a shirt, places it with the rest on the table, wipes her hands on her pinafore and goes to the door.

Yes?

We can't see who she is talking to, because the open door blocks the view.

Joe Kenny   Does Dick Hayes live here?

Freda pauses.

Freda   Yes. Why?

Joe Kenny   Is he in?

Freda   No. He's not come home yet. He's still at work.

Joe Kenny   Oh.

He pauses.

He said he was on nights this week. He said he'd be in.

Freda   He should have been but he's swopped shifts. His mother's on her last legs and he didn't want to be at work in case owt happened to her in t'night.

Joe Kenny   Oh. I see.

He pauses.

What time are you expecting him home then?

Freda looks across at the clock on the mantlepiece.

Freda   He shouldn't be long now. I've got his dinner on.

Joe Kenny   Can we wait for him then?

Freda pauses.

Freda	What do you want him for anyway?
Joe Kenny	We're scouts from Derby County. I'm Joe Kenny and this is George Hirst. We want him to come to Derby for a trial.
Freda	Oh. Well you'd better come in then.

She steps back to allow the two men to enter. As they step inside they take their caps off and wipe their boots on the mat. They are both dressed in overcoats, and are both wearing collars and ties. They knock the rain off their caps by banging them on their thighs, and shake the rain off their coats by shaking the lapels. Freda looks out as she closes the door.

It's still at it then?

Joe Kenny	At it? It's raining twice. It'd be a grand day for a funeral would this.
Freda	My heart dropped a mile when I saw you standing there. I thought you were from t'pit. I thought summat had happened to him.
Joe Kenny	Our hearts dropped a mile an' all when we got off that bus and they told us how far we'd to walk in this lot.
Freda	Which bus did you come on?
Joe Kenny	We caught one at Sheffield Lane Top to Hoyland.

Freda nods.

Freda   It's a fair walk from Hoyland. Here, sit down, you must be worn out.

She takes a washing basket off one of the chairs.

If you can get down that is. You couldn't have come on a worse day.

They sit down on two dining chairs, one behind the door and the other one next to the dresser, so that the door is between them. They look very incongruous and formal in their overcoats amongst the steamy chaos of the washday. They look as though they are waiting in a Doctor's surgery.

	Does he know you're coming?
Joe Kenny	We had a word with him after the match at Thorpe on Saturday.
Freda	Oh.
Joe Kenny	We'd seen him play a few times before that though. We'd never let on who we were though, just in case it put him off his game.
Freda	Do you think he's good enough to be a footballer? A professional footballer I mean?
George Hirst	He could be.
Joe Kenny	Oh, he's good enough. Don't you bother about that missus. He's a natural.
Freda	They all say that. They all say that he's a good player. His dad says that when he was three years old he could throw a ball up between his heels and catch it on his foot when it came down.
George Hirst	It's not music hall turns we're after. You need more than a bit of juggling to make the grade as a pro footballer.
Joe Kenny	He's a natural though, George. You've only to see him running with the ball. It stands out a mile.
Freda	He takes after his dad they say. He was a centre forward as well.
Joe Kenny	It's often the case. Centre forwards are born not made. Just like scholars. And Royalty.

Freda carries on with her work. She puts the clothes line up in the kitchen. There are four hooks in the corners of the ceiling. She fastens it round these to make a square, then crosses it diagonally across the centre of the ceiling. When she gets to the corner where the two men are sitting, she asks Joe Kenny to stand up for her so that she can use his chair to stand on to fasten the line to the hook. She talks as she works.

Freda	He scores a lot of goals don't he? Not that I know much about it. He never tells me owt. It's his dad

|||who tells me. I go round and do a bit of cleaning up now that his mother's bad.

Joe Kenny   That's what we want him for. He's one of them players who'll score goals whatever league he plays in.

Freda hangs up the whites, which she has placed in a pile on the table. She then washes the towels, scrubbing them, rubbing them up and down the rubbing board and wringing them out ready for the boiler. She then empties this tub outside, tilting it up on its rim and rolling it. The two men have to stand up and move their chairs to let her get out of the door. They know she is coming back in so they hold their chairs up waiting for her. When she returns from the outside grate rolling the empty tub, Joe Kenny closes the door after her and both men sit down again.

Freda then takes the steaming sheets out of the boiler with the stick and bowl, rinses and peggies them round in the rinsing tub, wrings them out through the mangle and hangs them up on the line. She uses the lengths of line across the back and down one side of the room so that they will be out of the way. Joe Kenny has to stand up for her again so that she can stand on his chair to arrange one of the sheets over the line.

Freda   I'm sorry it's not very comfortable, but I'll have to get done. I can't have a house like a tip when Dick comes in.

George Hirst   What time did you say he'd be back?

Freda looks at the clock.

Freda   He should be back anytime now. I'm going to mix his puddings in a minute.

George Hirst unbuttons his overcoat, takes out his pocket watch, studies it, then replaces it and buttons up his overcoat.

Do you want a cup of tea while you're waiting? You must be frozen to the marrow if you've come all that way in this lot.

The two men look at each other. George Hirst nods.

Joe Kenny Well, if it's not too much trouble, it'd come in very nicely thank you.

Freda takes the kettle off the hob, shakes it, looks inside, fills it then replaces it. She gives the fire a poke to hurry the kettle up.

Freda Where is it anyway, Derby?

Joe Kenny thinks for a moment.

Joe Kenny It's about forty miles from here I should say, wouldn't you, George?

George Hirst Fifty. Fifty'd be nearer the mark.

Freda It's a fair stretch then isn't it? How do you get there?

Joe Kenny From here? You walk it to Hoyland. Then you catch a bus to Sheffield Lane Top. From there you catch a tram to the station. Then you catch a train to Derby.

Freda It's a right trek isn't it?

Joe Kenny You've never been to Derby then?

Freda Never been! I've only been to Sheffield twice and that was to see my mother in hospital. Once when she lost our Betty, and once when she had that growth removed from her neck.

She adds several ladling cans of water to the boiler, drops the towels in and adds soap powder and soda. By this time the kettle is boiling and she makes a pot of tea.

Do you both want sugar?

Joe Kenny Three for me please, missus. And you can put it in with a number five shovel if you've got one.

George Hirst Just one for me.

He watches her.

That's enough.

Freda stirs both cups and hands them to the men.

Freda He never said you were coming.

George Hirst We arranged it after the match. We didn't have time to talk because we'd a train to catch.

Freda He never said owt when he got home.

She pauses.

He said that the centre half had been clogging him death all game. His shins were black and blue when he washed his legs to go out on Saturday night.

Joe Kenny Oh, he gets some clog iron, there's no doubt about that.

Freda speaks to herself while working.

Freda Mind you, he never does tell me owt. He's never in to tell me is he?

Joe Kenny He's got to expect it though, hasn't he? They're not going to stand there and let him run past 'em are they?

Freda is now washing the coloureds (pinafores, coloured shirts). She is using the tub that had previously been used for rinsing, after adding a few ladling cans of boiling water from the boiler. She scrubs them, rubs them up and down the rubbing board, wrings them out with her hands and places them in a pile on the table.

Freda His dad says he asks for it sometimes. He says he tries to make mugs out of 'em. He says that he's got too much old buck.

Joe Kenny Oh, he's cheeky alright.

George Hirst Cocky.

Freda I know. That's his trouble.

She pauses.

Clever Dick. That's what they used to call him at school. Nobody can tell him owt.

Joe Kenny Nobody had to tell him how to get that ball into the back of the net, that is a certainty.

Freda pokes the fire, then opens the little iron door of the boiler and pokes that fire as well. She goes into the pantry and down the steps into the cellar where the coal is kept. We hear the sound of shovelling, then she comes up carrying a large shovelful of coal, two-handed. She mends the boiler fire and repeats the journey down to the cellar and mends the other fire. She returns the shovel to the pantry top and brings out the ingredients to make the Yorkshire puddings.

George Hirst How old is your husband, Mrs Hayes?

Freda pauses.

Freda Twenty-two. Just.

George Hirst He must have been approached before by other clubs.

Freda pours some flour into a basin, cracks an egg into it and beats it up with a spoon. She acts as though she has not heard the question.

I mean, it's not as though he's still a lad, or that nobody's ever seen him play. He's well-known for miles around here. He's a marked man every time he steps out on to that field.

Joe Kenny We couldn't believe it first time we saw him. We'd had these reports from our local scout. 'Come up and see this Dick Hayes,' he kept saying. 'Come up and see him before it's too late. He's another Steve Bloomer,' he said.

He now speaks to George Hirst.

Can you remember that dummy he sold that centre half, George?

George Hirst nods.

Talk about send a man the wrong way. He finished up amongst the supporters against them lav walls down the far side.

George Hirst He should have shot then though, instead of trying to dribble it round the goalie.

Joe Kenny It was only the mud that stopped him though, George. He was round the goalie. He'd have left him on a dry day.

George Hirst But it wasn't a dry day. He was trying to do too much. He'd have scored with a shot.

Joe Kenny He did get two though, George. Be fair.
George Hirst I know, but they lost didn't they?
Freda mixes the pudding batter.
Freda One or two blokes have been to see him. They used to go to his mothers an'all before we were married.
George Hirst Where from?
Freda Local clubs mainly – Sheffield, Barnsley, Huddersfield. He should have gone to Sheffield Wednesday once for a trial but he never got off.
George Hirst Why?
Freda He didn't get up in time and he missed the train.
She pauses.
That was when he was still living at home though.
Freda goes to the hearth and lifts the cloth on a pancheon of dough. She prods it with her finger, then replaces the cloth. She opens the oven door and with a tea towel, takes out a pan of hash to see if it is done. She puts it back and closes the oven door.
Freda I wish he would go.
Joe Kenny Go? Where?
Freda Derby. Anywhere.
Joe Kenny It's a good club. He'd be well looked after.
Freda greases the tins ready to put the Yorkshire pudding mixture in.
Freda How much would he get paid?
She looks at the clock again.
Just wait a minute will you?
She picks up the poker and bangs three times on the fire back. Then she fills a large pan with water and puts it to boil on the gas ring. There is a knock on the door, and Winnie, the next-door neighbour, pops her head round the door.
Winnie Do you want me, love?
Freda Is your Stanley still off school, Winnie?

Winnie Why, do you want him?

Freda Will you ask him to run down to the Queen's for me and ask Ernest if Dick's there? If he is, will you tell him he's to come straight home, as there's two men from Derby come to see him?

Winnie has a good look at the two men before she goes.

Winnie I'll send him straight away.

She goes out closing the door behind her.

Freda He sometimes calls for a drink before he comes home.

Joe Kenny You need one I can tell you. I know, I've worked down there.

He pauses.

When I first started down the pit the pubs were open all day. Ike Johnson who kept the Acorn used to be open when the night men came off at six. He used to have all the pints half pulled on the bar, then start filling them up when he heard the clogs coming up the lane.

He pauses again.

One morning he laid too long and he wasn't up. We were all outside banging on the door and shouting. Joe Jones picked some muck up and threw it up against the bedroom window. 'Hey up!' he shouted. 'Are you stopping in bed all day then, or what?'

He shakes his head and smiles to himself as he remembers.

He was a bugger was Joe.

He pauses.

He got crushed between two tubs.

Freda He'll not be long. The Queen's only a cock stride away. You'll have passed it on t' corner on your way up.

George Hirst I hope not. We've a train to catch at half past five.

Two Men from Derby

Freda looks at the clock again. She pours the pudding mixture into the two tins and puts them into the oven. It is as though she is hoping that this action itself will bring her husband home from wherever he is. She starts to fill the empty tub with ladling cans of cold water from the tap. Then there is a knock on the door.

Freda That'll be Stanley. Come in, love.

A ten-year-old boy comes in and stands uncertainly just inside the door. He leaves the door open, ready to retreat. The two men sitting either side of the door do not make it any easier for him because they both sit staring at him, waiting to hear what he has to say.

Is he there, love?

Stanley No, Mr Turner says he's gone.

Freda Did he say where to?

Stanley No, he just said he'd gone out.

Freda pauses.

Freda Well. Will you run up to the Hare and Hounds for me then love, and see if he's in there?

Stanley nods and runs out. Joe Kenny has to close the door after him. Freda looks at the window.

Come straight back and tell me won't you, Stanley?

She pauses.

He sometimes calls in the Hare and Hounds instead of the Queen's.

George Hirst Does he sometimes call in them both?

Freda does not answer and goes back to ladling cold water into the tub. Then she looks at the pancheon of dough again.

Freda How much did you say he'd get paid?

Joe Kenny It depends. At his age he'd probably start on about eight pounds a week. But if he stopped with the club and did well, after a few years he could be bringing home owt up to fifteen pounds with bonuses.

Freda Fifteen pounds a week! Just for playing at football?

Joe Kenny Better than the pit isn't it, missus? How much is he getting there, three or four pounds a week?

Freda I don't know. He don't tell me. He just gives me my housekeeping and keeps t'rest for himself.

Joe Kenny Well it'll not be above five, I can tell you that.

He pauses.

Then there's a free house of course, and he'd travel about a lot ...

Freda A free house?

Joe Kenny Rent free I mean; well, nearly. A club house, we don't give it to you, I don't mean that.

Freda What sort of house? What are they like inside?

Joe Kenny What sort? I don't know. What sort of houses are they, George?

George Hirst is not interested in houses. He is taking his watch out again. Joe Kenny has to answer the question himself. He looks around the room.

Bigger than this. A bathroom. Nowt fancy mind. But nice; in town.

Freda It sounds lovely.

Joe Kenny Oh, they're looked after alright, are our players. It's a good club. It's got a good record. We were Division 1 runners up in 1895–96, and last season. Division 2 champions 1911–12, 1914–15, and runners up in 1925–26. We've been F.A. Cup finalists three times, 1898, 1899 and 1903. And we've had some great players. There was the immortal Steve Bloomer of course, who played 20 times for England, and altogether scored 297 goals for Derby. Then there's Jack Bowers playing now. He looks as though he might even beat Steve's individual total this season; he's got 27 goals already ...

Freda It sounds lovely. I've always wanted to live in a town.

Joe Kenny Don't get carried away, Missus. It wouldn't be

	Buckingham Palace. We're not the Arsenal. Not yet anyway.
Freda	No, but it'd be better than this hole, wouldn't it?
	Joe Kenny looks around to confirm there is no disputing this fact. But as it would be insulting to say so, he keeps quiet.
	Owt'd be better than being stuck in here all day. And I wouldn't be washing these any more either, would I?
	She picks up her husband's pit clothes, shirt, vest and drawers, and throws them individually into the tub in which she has previously washed the coloureds.
Joe Kenny	You're better off washing 'em than wearing 'em, I can tell you that. If you'd to go down there six days a week you'd be thankful for what you've got. You're better off filling washing tubs than coal tubs, believe me.
	There is a little knock on the door.
Freda	Come in, Stanley!
	(*Stanley comes in. He is panting this time. He is just as apprehensive as last time. The two men stare at him again, waiting for him to speak.*)
	Is he there?
Stanley	No. They say he's not been in.
Freda	Has anybody seen him?
Stanley	I don't know. I didn't ask 'em all.
Freda	Alright love.
	She pauses.
	Now then. If I give you a penny will you run to the Prince, the Star and the Club, and ask there for me?
	She pauses.
	Do you know where they are?
Stanley	Club. I don't know where that is.
Freda	Down Fitzwilliam Street. That big red brick building near the bottom.

Stanley pauses while he works it out.

Stanley Do you mean near where my uncle Walter lives? Where that bowling green is over their back wall?

Freda That's it, love.

She takes her purse out of the cupboard and finds him a penny. Before she lets him go, she crouches down in front of him and gets hold of his arms. By this action she hopes that she will convey her own sense of seriousness and urgency to the boy.

Now then, tell me where you're going, love.

Stanley speaks haltingly as he remembers the names.

Stanley Prince. Star. Club.

Freda And what are you going to say?

Stanley I'm going to say. Has anybody seen Mr Hayes? And if he's there, he's to come straight home 'cos there's two men to see him.

Freda That's a good lad. Two men from Derby Football Club tell him.

Joe Kenny Derby County Football Club.

Stanley nods and turns to leave the house.

George Hirst Wait a minute lad.

George feels in his pockets, brings out some loose change and selects a penny. He leans across to the boy showing him the full coin by holding the bottom rim between his forefinger and thumb.

And there's another penny for you if you look sharp.

He does not give the penny to Stanley, but places it deliberately on the corner of the table.

Freda Off you go now, love.

When he has gone, Joe Kenny has to stand up and close the door after him again. Freda calls after him.

Don't be long will you, Stanley?

George Hirst He'd better not be, or we'll have gone by the time he gets back.

Freda	Can't you catch a later train?
George Hirst	There isn't a later train. We've to be on that ten to four bus from Hoyland or we'll miss it.

Freda starts to soap and scrub the pit clothes in the tub.

Freda	Men. You can't rely on 'em for two minutes together.

She takes it out of the pit clothes, rubbing them viciously up and down the rubbing board. Joe Kenny nodding at her and grinning, makes an oblique reference to her pregnancy.

Joe Kenny	You can rely on 'em for one thing, that is a certainty.
Freda	Ar, and that's about all.
Joe Kenny	Get away with you. You don't know you're born.
Freda	You what! Stuck in here all day washing and ironing and cooking and cleaning. Never going anywhere week in week out. What sort of life do you call that?
Joe Kenny	And where do you think your husband goes every day, to a picnic? I know. I've worked down there.

He pauses.

I can remember when I was playing for Huddersfield and we looked like going down one year. I went home to see my mother after we'd played at Notts. County and I called in a pub that I used to go in before I left home. As soon as they saw me they were at it, having me on, making fun of me. How did we go on against such and such? How many goals had I let in against so and so? One bloke shouted across, you look like going down if you're not careful, Joe. Ar, I said, but it'll still be better than going down the pit.

Freda takes the towels out of the boiler with the stick and bowl and drops them into the tub containing the clean rinsing water. She peggies them, wrings them out through the mangle and hangs them up on the clothes line. The hasty, rough way she is handling the clothes betrays the anger and frustration she is feeling.

Freda I know, but at least when you've finished your shift, you've finished for the day. I've never done. And it'll get worse. I'm expecting a bairn in three months, and if everybody round here's owt to go by it'll not be the last either. It'll be the same old tale, stuck here for ever with a cartload of kids growing up round me.

Joe Kenny Everybody else has to put up with it.

Freda You don't put up with it. My mother always said that if men and women had babies in turns and t'men had theirs first, there wouldn't be a family in this country bigger than two.

She pauses.

She was right an' all. What do men know about it? They bring their money home on a Friday and they think that's it. It's dinner, washed, changed and out. The next time you see 'em's either in bed stinking of beer, or next morning when they're shaking you awake to get up and get their breakfasts.

Joe Kenny A man's got to have some enjoyment when he's been at work all day. He'd go mad if he didn't.

Freda And what about a woman? Don't she? Don't she work all day?

Joe Kenny I know; but that's different. That's woman's work. A woman's used to it, isn't she?

Freda A woman has to be, don't she? Look at Dick. He's a good husband. He works hard. I'm not saying owt about him. And don't think I don't know owt about t'pit, my dad and all five brothers were colliers. I was brought up with it. But we've only been married a few months and I hardly see owt of him already.

She pauses.

I don't know why men bother getting married, honestly. He sees more of his mates than he sees of me. He's swapped houses that's all. Instead of his mother feeding and seeing to him, I'm doing it instead.

Two Men from Derby

Joe Kenny   What do you expect him to do when he comes home, just stop in all night.

Freda   I do.

Joe Kenny   I know you do.

He sounds exasperated now.

But that's different.

Freda   Why is it? Why don't he spend a bit more time with me, instead of wanting to be out boozing every night with his mates?

Joe Kenny   Because he needs to. When you've been down that hole all day you need to get out a bit. You need to get a few pints down you to make you forget. You've got to compensate. You've got to make the best out of them few hours that you can call your own. They might be the last you'll get.

George Hirst   I think your puddings are done, missus.

Freda rushes to the oven, opens the door and takes the tins out with a cloth. They are overdone, but still edible.

Freda   They'll soften up when they get some gravy on 'em.

She takes the pan of hash out of the oven as well and places it on the oven top with the Yorkshire puddings.

Where the hell is he? It's time he was home now.

Joe Kenny   They'll save a bit won't they?

Freda   You know why he's late don't you?

George Hirst   Why?

Freda   Because it's wash day and it's raining. He hates coming home when t'house is all upset and there's washing hanging up everywhere.

Joe Kenny   You can't blame him for wanting a bit of comfort when he's been where he has for eight hours, can you?

Freda   No, and you can't blame me because this house isn't big enough to swing a cat round, and I've nowhere else to hang things up in.

Joe Kenny I'm not blaming anybody, missus.

Freda So he stops out drinking. Or he slopes off somewhere with one of his mates for an hour or two and leaves his dinner spoiling on the oven top.

Joe Kenny It's a hard life.

Freda You're not kidding mister. Look at my mother. What did she ever get out of life? Furthest she ever went was an outing now and again to Locke Park at Barnsley. Do you know, she reckoned it up once, and she said for three years the furthest she ever went was to Titus Healey's shop at the end of our street. What sort of life was that.

She pauses.

Look at Dick's mother. She had to get married when she was eighteen. She was forty-two years old when she had their Clarice. Twenty-four years of married life and she still hadn't done with it. Look at her now. On her death bed. A lifetime spent bringing kids up. She's had no life of her own at all.

She pauses.

And talk about bitter. She might be dying but she's still got a tongue like an adder. What a temper. Dick's dad was that late home one dinner time that she ran up to the Hare and Hounds in her pinny with his plate in her hand and plonked it down on t'table in front of him.

She pauses.

And do you know what he said?

Joe Kenny What?

Freda Have you put any salt on it?

Joe Kenny laughs. George Hirst manages a smile.

When she goes, she'd take him with her if she could.

Freda now rinses and peggies the coloureds. She wrings them out through the mangle and hangs them on the line. The clothes line is nearly full now and it makes the room look even smaller.

Well, I don't want that carry on all my life. I want to go somewhere, and do summat with my life.

Joe Kenny The Club'll not provide you with a maid you know, if you come to Derby.

Freda I know that. I don't want a maid. But things'd be different if we could get away from here.

She pauses.

At least I'd be sure he'd be coming home every day, wouldn't I? There's not that many men get killed playing at football.

She serves her husband's dinner and puts the plate in the oven top to keep it warm.

And he wouldn't be able to go out drinking as much, would he, if he was a footballer? He'd have to train and get fit wouldn't he?

George Hirst Does he smoke?

Freda pauses.

Freda Sometimes.

George Hirst Heavy?

Freda No. He can't afford it.

George Hirst Fatal. Smoking and drinking for an athlete.

Freda He might not want to go out all the time then though, mightn't he? He'd be happier in his work. He might want to spend a bit more time at home. That makes sense don't it?

She pauses. Both men sit and look at her without answering. There is a knock on the door. Winnie pops her head in.

Winnie Has our Stanley come back yet, Freda?

Freda Yes. I've just sent him up t'Hare and Hounds to see if Dick's in there.

Winnie I thought he was a long time.

She pauses.

You haven't found him yet then?

Freda He'll be here in a minute. His dinner's served out ready.

Winnie I don't know. You want to take a firm hold of him, make him settle down before it's too late. How long have you been married, five months? And …

Freda Seven. Seven months.

Winnie Seven months, a bairn on the way and he's at it already. Out at all hours, rolling home singing and shouting. Missing his dinner. Our Walter's been home an hour now.

Freda I'll send your Stanley round as soon as he gets back then.

Winnie You've got to be firm with 'em. Let 'em know who's t'boss. They'll have you up a stick if you let 'em.

There is a moment's silence in the house.

Is there owt else I can do for you, Freda.

Freda No. Not just now. I'll send your Stanley in as soon as he comes back.

Winnie Right love. If there's owt else you want, just give me a knock.

She goes out, closing the door behind her. Freda waits until she hears Winnie's door bang before she speaks.

Freda Their Walter. He's nowt but a doormat. Anybody'll tell you that.

George Hirst At least she knows where he is.

Freda She's just jealous that's all. Their Walter. Who'd want to be married to an article like that?

Freda takes the pit clothes out of the tub, wrings them out through the mangle and throws them into the rinsing tub. She then scrubs the pit socks, which are thick with muck, up and down the rubbing board.

George Hirst Why hasn't he ever signed for anybody, Mrs Hayes?

Two Men from Derby

She carries on working as though she has not heard the question.

He can play a bit you know.

Freda   I know that. He knows it an'all.

She pauses.

But he don't take it seriously. He don't take owt seriously.

Joe Kenny   I can't understand that when his only other choice is the pit.

Freda   I know, but he won't budge from round here. He gets ten shillings a match for Saturday afternoons. He doesn't have to train. He's proud of that, not having to train. He thinks it's clever. He's got his mates. And his beer. And he's got me to see to him.

She pauses.

I think he's scared of risking it just in case he fails.

Joe Kenny   He can always come back if he don't make it.

Freda   No.

She pauses.

It's easier to think that you could have made it, than to know that you didn't.

George Hirst does not answer him.

Joe Kenny   Well, we think he could make it don't we, George?

Freda   I wish you'd try and tell him that.

George Hirst   That's what we came for, but it looks as though we've backed a loser.

Freda   Oh no. Don't say that. He might listen to you. I mean, it's a long way to come from Derby. It might make him think again.

George Hirst   We're not going to have time to make him think owt, unless he comes home in the next few minutes.

Freda puts her husband's dinner plate back in the oven.

Freda   He'll be in anytime now. He's bound to be.

George Hirst takes his watch out and looks at it again.

George Hirst That kid's taking his time isn't he?

Joe Kenny He's probably spent that penny and buggered off. I bet he's stood up an entry with his finger stuck into a bag of Kali or summat.

Freda No, he wouldn't do that. He's a good lad. He does as he's told does young Stanley.

She pauses.

Do you want another pot of tea while you're waiting. I'll pop t'kettle on and mash some fresh.

George Hirst No thanks, missus. We haven't got time.

Freda Well I'll just try and get done then, ready for when he comes in.

She peggies the pit clothes in the rinsing tub, wrings them out through the mangle and puts them on the table ready to hang up. There is a knock on the door. Joe Kenny immediately stands up and lets Stanley in. He is panting heavily.

Did you find him, love?

Stanley pauses to get his breath back.

Stanley No, he'd been in the Star, but he'd gone.

Freda Did they know where to?

Stanley No. They said he'd gone out with Mr Mott.

Freda I'll give him Mr Mott when he comes in.

Stanley He'd not been anywhere else though.

Freda Did you try their house?

Stanley Whose house?

Freda Tommy Mott's.

Stanley No. You didn't ask me to go there.

Freda He could be there. Or he could be down t'gardens at Tommy's pigeon hut.

George Hirst It sounds as though you're married to the Scarlet Pimpernel to me, missus. He could be here. He could be there. He could be anywhere by the sounds of it.

He stands up. Then Joe Kenny stands up.

Two Men from Derby

Freda You're not going yet, are you? It'll not take him a minute to run down to Tommy's house, and then to t'gardens.

George Hirst We haven't got time. We'll miss that bus if we stop any longer.

Freda It'll not take him a minute.

George Hirst The lad'll be worn to a frazzle if he does any more running. Look at him. He's like a skinned rabbit as it is.

Freda He doesn't mind, do you love? He's always running errands for me.

George Hirst No. After all, missus, he did know we were coming.

Freda He's had to swap shifts. I told you that. You can't blame him for that can you?

George Hirst I'm not blaming him for owt. But I said we'd come Tuesday dinner time, and he said he'd be in.

Freda He's probably got t'wrong day. Perhaps he thinks you're coming another day.

George Hirst I wouldn't think so. It doesn't take much remembering from Saturday to Tuesday does it?

Freda Perhaps he's forgot. He's got a lot on his mind you know. What with his mother badly and all that.

George Hirst He doesn't seem to be worrying too much about her anyroad. I notice you haven't sent the lad round to see if he's called in there.

Freda I can do though. That's where he probably is. It's only in the next street. Stanley ...?

George Hirst No. Don't bother, lad. We've no time now.

Both men put on their caps and prepare to leave. Joe Kenny speaks to Stanley.

Joe Kenny Is it still raining, son?

(*He feels at Stanley's hair.*)

Either that or you're sweating heavy.

Freda What shall I tell him when he comes in?

George Hirst	Tell him that we came to see him like we said we would.
Freda	Can I arrange for him to see you sometime? Perhaps he could come to Sheffield to see you? He's on days next week. He could come one afternoon.
George Hirst	We'll let you know.
Freda	Will you come and watch him again?
George Hirst	We've no need to watch him anymore. We know enough about him now.
Freda	Will you come back?
George Hirst	I don't know. We've a lot of players to see. A lot of reports to follow up. We'll let you know if we want to come up again.

He opens the door.

Joe Kenny	Thanks for the tea, missus.

He looks outside.

We'll get drenched walking to the bus stop.

George Hirst	We'll get drenched if we miss it and have to walk to Sheffield Lane Top.

They leave the house. Joe Kenny speaks from outside.

Joe Kenny	Ta-ra Mrs Hayes. We might see you again sometime.

She watches them walk away for a few moments, then closes the door behind them. She is furious and bitter.

Freda	Just wait. Just wait 'til he comes in.

When she turns round from the door, she sees Stanley looking at her. She has forgotten about him.

You'd better go home now, love. Your mam'll be wondering where you are.

Stanley	Can I have that other penny now?
Freda	What other penny?

Stanley points to the coin that George Hirst had placed on the corner of the table.

Stanley	That one. He said I could have it if I hurried up.

Freda Of course you can have it.
Stanley picks up the penny.
Stanley I went as fast as I could.
Freda I know you did love. It wasn't your fault.
She opens the door for him.
And dry your hair when you get in. I don't want you catching your death of cold on my account.
She closes the door after him and goes across to the hearth.
Just wait 'til he gets in. I'll kill him. I will. I'll murder him. It's not fair on him. It's just not right.
She grabs hold of the tub in which she has just washed the pit socks and wheels it outside. There is a pause while she empties it. Then she hurries in, leaving the tub outside.
And if he thinks he's having his dinner in this house, he's another think coming.
She takes his dinner out of the oven and slings it on to the fire. Then she throws the extra Yorkshire pudding on, and the rest of the hash out of the pan.
Football. I'll give him bloody football.
She goes to the bottom cupboard by the fireplace, rummages around inside, pulling out the odd shoe in the process, until she finds his football boots. They are stiff and still caked with last Saturday's dry mud. One at a time she throws them on to the fire. Because the fire has been damped down by all the food they do not take light. She stands there, looking at them. Then, when they start to smoke she panics, picks up the poker and knocks them into the hearth. She picks them up, takes them to the sink copper and puts them both under the tap. Then she wipes them down with a floorcloth and inspects them. There is no damage done, so she puts them back into the bottom cupboard and closes the doors.

Shooting Stars

Barry Hines
Adapted for schools by Lawrence Till

LIST OF CHARACTERS

Gary Gibson
Sean Gibson
Vic (a West Indian)
Paula Gibson (Gary and Sean's mother)
Alison Connor
Sue
Christine
Bob Southgate (City Director)
Jim Price (City Manager)
Calvin Clark (West Indian footballer)
Karl Gutke (Hamburg Manager)
Simmons
Electrical shop manager
Mr Groves
Cleaner
Paul Reid (Calvin's friend at City)
DJ
City Player
Night Club manager
Waiter
Zoe
Two women at Night Club
A drunk
Robert Mitchell (a friend of Gary's)
Hotel Receptionist
Two girls at Bus Station
Lost Property Office attendant
Reporter
Detective Miller
Detective Stone
Chinese takeaway owner
Armed police
Doctors

SHOOTING STARS

Outside the City Football stadium on Match Day.

All the streets and patches of wasteland surrounding the stadium are filled with cars. Three boys – Gary, his younger brother Sean, and their friend, Vic – break into one of the cars. They search the pockets of an overcoat in the back seat. Gary opens the glove compartment and takes out an object wrapped in cloth. When he opens it, he reveals a hand gun. The boys are wide-eyed with excitement as they pass it round.

* *

Four friends, Paula Gibson (late thirties), Alison Connor (18), Christine (early twenties), Sue (early thirties) are walking down a crowded street towards the City stadium. They are keen supporters and attend every home game.
They buy programmes, then pay at the turnstiles and enter the ground. Sue, who is on the large side, has difficulty squeezing through the turnstile which amuses her friends.

* *

Sean is hanging around in the car park before the game, looking in car windows and trying the occasional door handle. We can hear music from inside the ground. Bob Southgate, the City Chairman, drives up in his car and parks in one of the reserved spaces behind the main stand. Sean sidles up to the car. Southgate gets out. In the back seat we can see a massive Rottweiler.

Sean Look after your car, mister?

Southgate disdainfully, points at the Rottweiler in the back seat.

Southgate He looks after my car.

Southgate walks towards the Players and Officials entrance in the stand. Then, just as he is about to go in:

Sean Hey, mister!

Southgate turns round.

Does he blow your tyres up as well?

Southgate grins appreciating Sean's cheek.

Southgate Here ...

Southgate takes a pound coin out of his pocket and flicks it to Sean.

Sean Thanks, mister.

Southgate enters the ground shaking his head in amusement at Sean's enterprise.

* *

Inside the City football stadium. The changing room on Match Day.

The City players are getting changed. One of the players is lying on the treatment table having his leg massaged by the physiotherapist. The manager, Jim Price, is working his way round the room having a quiet word of encouragement with individual players. He approaches

Shooting Stars

Calvin Clark who is of West Indian origin, and the club's star player, leading scorer and English international.

Price   Okay, son?

Calvin   Yeah. Fine.

Price   Watch the off-sides. They come out like whippets this lot.

Calvin nods and continues to lace up his boots.

And Conroy'll be taking no prisoners, so watch yourself.

Calvin   Yeah, I know. I've still got the bruises from last time.

Price   Ignore him son. That's the best way to deal with him.

* *

Outside the City stadium on Match Day.

Paula, Alison, Sue and Christine are standing in the crowd behind the goal waiting for the teams to appear. The women are looking at their programmes. Alison turns to the player's profile in her programme. This week's player is Calvin Clark. Underneath his photograph there is a list of his favourite things.

Alison   Guess what Calvin's favourite food is?

Sue   Steak and chips.

Alison has trouble with the pronunciation.

Alison   Coq-au-Vin.

She pauses.

What's that?

Sue   Chicken cooked in wine.

Alison   Favourite drink?

Christine   Lager.

Alison   Burgundy.

She pauses.
I thought that was a place.
Paula I hope his wife's a good cook.
Alison He's not married.
The City team run out onto the pitch. The four women cheer and applaud with the other supporters. We pick out Calvin as he runs towards the goal at the Kop end. The crowd chant his name. Calvin waves in recognition. We see shots of the match in progress featuring Calvin Clark. These are intercut with shots of Karl Gutke, the Manager of Hamburg F.C. (an attractive, charismatic man, dressed in expensive clothes) and Bob Southgate, the Manager of City F.C. and some other directors are watching from one of the glass fronted executive boxes overlooking the pitch. Paula and Alison are on the Kop. The telephone rings. Southgate picks it up. Southgate speaks into the phone.

Southgate Hello Clive ... They've what? Is it serious? Yes, yes, I know they will. Vultures. Stall them. Tell them what you like. Tell them it's a routine enquiry and there's nothing to worry about ... . Okay, Clive? Just keep calm. The last thing we want to do is panic the shareholders ... We're losing three-one.

He looks worried as he puts down the telephone.

Gutke Good control ... . Lays it off well to bring in the wingman ... .
Southgate He's got good feet. Good first touch ... . Yes! Brave header! He is not afraid to go in where it hurts.
Gutke How many goals has he scored this season?
Southgate Twenty-three.
Gutke You think he can do that for us?
Southgate He'll score goals anywhere.
Gutke He's the man I want.

* *

Shooting Stars

The City Centre on Match Day.

While the match is in progress, Gary is walking through the City Centre. He sees Simmons and goes up to him.

Gary   Hey, Simmons. What were you up to with Alison Connor the other night?

Simmons   What do you mean?

Gary   You know. In the Aquarius. Chatting her up and that.

Simmons   We were just dancing that's all.

Gary   Yeah. I know your game. Well, just keep away from her.

Simmons stands up sensing trouble.

Simmons   What's it to you, anyway? She's not your bird.

Gary   Never mind whose bird she is. Just keep away from her right!

Gary nudges and pushes him on his way. He then practises a few karate kicks at Simmons without making contact. We can then see that he is good at the sport. Simmons walks away, glancing back in a sullen, hostile manner.

Simmons   You'll get it Gibson! Just you wait!

Gary makes as if to run after him, but Simmons disappears amongst the crowd of shoppers. Gary meets up with Sean.

* *

Gary and Sean approach an electrical good's shop. They stop and look at the football results on the television sets in the window.

Sean   Look, City have lost, again.

Gary	That means Mum'll be in a bad mood again.
Sean	We'd better keep out of her way till she gets over it.

* *

Gary and Sean enter an electrical goods shop.

Sean looks at record players and ghetto blasters, then stops in front of a television next to Vic (aged 17) a black youth, who is watching a report on the football results. The Commentator speaks.

Commentator ... Another two goals from Calvin Clark brings his total for the season to twenty-five. Unfortunately, Clark's goals could not prevent City from slipping to yet another defeat and they are now sliding perilously close to the relegation zone ...

As Vic and Sean watch the match report, Gary enters the shop in the background.

Vic	Brilliant that Clark.
Sean	You what? He's rubbish.
Vic	One of the best players in Europe.
Sean	I've seen better players on a Subbuteo pitch.
Vic	Why don't you shut your mouth?
Sean	Make me.

The discrepancy between the antagonists is absurd. Not only is Vic much older than Sean, he is also much taller and heavier. The argument attracts the attention of other customers in the shop.

Vic pushes Sean who retaliates and they begin to scuffle, attracting the attention of the shop assistants who rush forward and try and separate them.

With all eyes on the fight, Gary picks up a video camera and walks calmly out of the shop.

The shop manager and assistants separate Vic and Sean and bundle them towards the door.

Manager Go on! And if I see you in here again, I'll call the police.

The assistants push the two boys into the street. Vic and Sean walk away in opposite directions, glancing back at each other.

* *

A city backstreet at night after the match.

Gary, Sean and Vic are approaching a pub. Gary has his arms across his chest, supporting the stolen video camera concealed inside his bomber jacket. When they reach the pub, Gary transfers the camera to Vic then goes inside. Vic and Sean gaze admiringly at a Jaguar parked outside the pub, then bend down and look through the window at the dashboard.

* *

Inside a public house, the evening after the match.

Gary stands inside the door looking around. He spots a smartly dressed man in an overcoat sitting on his own, reading the local evening sports paper. Gary walks across to his table.

Gary Hello, Mr Groves.

Groves looks over the newspaper at him. He is an eminently respectable looking man in a pin-striped suit and polished shoes. He is smoking a cigar and drinking whisky.

Groves Good evening, Gary. Sit down.

Gary sits down.

Drink?

Gary shakes his head.

Cigar?

Gary No thanks. I've got to go.

(*He pauses and then speaks quietly.*)

We've got a camcorder. Brand new. J.V.C. Four hundred quid job.

Groves puts down the newspaper, takes out his wallet and discreetly counts out £150 in notes which he passes to Gary under the table. Gary puts them in his pocket.

Thanks.

He pauses.

Do you want any more blank cassettes?

Groves Definitely not. I've got enough cassettes to build Hadrian's Wall. And no more car radios for the time being. There's a glut on the market.

Gary Right.

He pauses.

Anything else?

Groves Yes.

He pauses.

School uniforms.

Gary What?

Groves Riverdale and Bloomfield particularly.

Gary Never heard of them.

Groves smirks.

Groves No, I don't suppose you have, Gary. They're private schools.

He pauses.

The uniform is an expensive item on top of the astronomical fees one has to pay for a decent education these days. I'll write down the details.

Groves takes out an expensive fountain pen and writes the details on a piece of paper. He gives it to Gary who reads it.

An unusual order I must admit. But in today's enterprise culture one must respond to the fluctuating demands of the market place.

Gary folds up the sheet of paper and puts it away.

Gary Do you want to buy a gun?

Groves looks at him in surprise.

Groves A gun? What kind of gun?

Gary A hand gun.

Groves Good Lord, no. Not my line at all. Far too dangerous. I'd get rid of it if I was you. Drop it in the canal or something before you get into trouble.

Gary shakes his head.

Gary It's too valuable for that.

Groves pauses.

Groves Look keep quiet about it and keep it hidden. I may be able to put you in touch with an interested party. Okay?

Gary nods. Groves slides his car keys across the table. Gary picks them up.

There's a case of champagne in the boot. Take a bottle if you like. It's non vintage but perfectly drinkable.

Gary stands up and leaves the pub. Groves watches him go, then goes back to his newspaper.

* *

Inside a derelict flat, the night after the match.

Gary, Vic and Sean have broken into a flat on the top floor of an abandoned block. They have scavenged items of furniture (a sofa, mattress and a couple of chairs) from the other flats and are sitting around drinking cans of lager, smoking and listening to music on a cassette recorder.

The windows are boarded up and the room is lit by a couple of candles. There is the unopened bottle of champagne on the window sill.

Gary is trying to rewind a cassette tape.

Vic Got any fags?

Both Gary's hands are occupied with the tape. He lifts an elbow to allow Vic to feel in his jacket pocket.

Gary In my pocket ...

Vic feels in his pocket, but instead of bringing out a packet of cigarettes, he produces a bottle of perfume.

Vic What's this then?

Gary is terribly embarrassed. He tries to snatch the bottle back but Vic evades his hand. He reads the label.

'Chanel No 5'. You've got expensive taste, man.

Gary Hey! Give it here!

Vic Who's it for then?

He knows full well.

Come on. Who's it for?

Gary tries to wrestle the bottle back.

Gary My mother. It's her birthday next week.

Sean speaks innocently.

Sean It's not. Mum's birthday's in November.

Vic laughs. Gary is furious.

Gary You shut your face!

Sean It is. It's on Bonfire Night.

Gary And get off home! I'm sick of your hanging round all the time.

Sean What for? I haven't done owt wrong!

Gary Go on! Get!

Gary pushes Sean across the room then pushes him out and locks the door. Sean hammers furiously on the door to be let back in. Vic enjoys all this enormously. He dabs a couple of drops of perfume behind his ears, then lies back on the sofa in an outrageously suggestive position.

Vic I'm ready for you darling.

Gary is not amused.

Gary And you can shut up an' all!

* *

A tunnel/corridor in the City stadium, the day after the match.

The City squad, including Calvin and Paul Reid, Calvin's closest friend at the club, are walking up the corridor towards the changing room. They are muddy and sweaty after a training session on the pitch. As they walk by the cleaner, she takes an autograph book out of her overall pocket.

Cleaner Excuse me Calvin, will you sign this for my neighbour's little boy?

Calvin Yeah. 'Course I will.

He takes the book and signs it.

Cleaner He's got all the stars in there. Cliff Richard, Jimmy Tarbuck.

Calvin laughs.

Calvin I'm in good company then, aren't I?

He hands back the book.

Cleaner He's a right little spiv though. He traces them and sells them to the kids at school.

Calvin He sounds as if he'll do well for himself.

Calvin and Paul continue along the corridor. As they reach the changing room, they are intercepted by Price leaving his office.

Price Calvin!

Calvin and Paul pause at the changing room door and wait for Price to approach. Price addressed Calvin.

I'd like to see you for a minute ...

Paul goes into the changing room. Price takes Calvin's arm and takes him to one side. He looks uneasy. He doesn't know where to start.

Everything okay son?

Calvin Yeah. Fine.

Price Your knee cleared up?

Calvin Yeah. It's still a bit sore but it's alright.

Price pauses.

Price I suppose you've heard about Mr Southgate's business problems?

Calvin Yeah. Something about an enquiry isn't it?

Price According to what I can gather, he's got a serious cash flow problem.

Calvin He's been terrific for the club, Mr Southgate. All that money he's put into it and that.

Price Yes. Well ... anyway, the long and the short of it is, Hamburg's come in for you and Mr Southgate's decided to accept their offer.

Calvin stares at him, stunned. He can't believe it. Players passing along the corridor glance at them. They can see that it is serious business.

Calvin What! I don't want to go to Hamburg!

Price Don't blame me son. I fought it tooth and nail at the Board Meeting, but they made an offer Mr Southgate couldn't refuse.

Calvin How much?

Price Three million.

Calvin gives a low whistle of astonishment.

We'll contact your agent. It'll secure your future son. You'll be set up for life.

Calvin pauses and looks troubled.

Calvin Yeah .... I'm happy here though. All my mates are here and that.

Price I know that and it'll break my heart to see you go. There's nothing we can do about it though. It's just business that's all. Prawns in the game son, that's all we are. Prawns in the game.

Calvin pauses.

Calvin I don't even know where Hamburg is.

* *

Inside the City stadium. The kitchen on day 3.

Calvin and Paul, dressed in tracksuits, are studying what appears to be a map on the table. The table also contains a large metal teapot, bottles of milk and mugs. Calvin and Paul are drinking tea. Paul is pointing out German towns.

Paul Hamburg ... Dusseldorf ... Berlin ... Munich.

A close-up reveals they are looking at a map of Germany.

Calvin I didn't realise that Berlin was that far east. It's nearly in Poland.

Paul I played in Berlin when I was at Chelsea. A reporter asked Johnny Kay what he thought of the wall. 'Not much' he said, 'when you've seen one wall you've seen 'em all.'

He laughs, then speaks seriously.

It'll be a good move for you Calvin. Hamburg are one of the top clubs in Europe. Karl Gutke's the manager. He played for Germany in the 1966 World Cup final.

Paul is upset that Calvin is leaving City. Calvin senses this and tries to cheer him up.

Calvin You'll be able to come over and see me.

* *

Inside an Asian video shop on day 3.

Alison, who works in the video shop, is replacing video cassettes on the shelves. One or two customers are browsing. Gary, Vic and Sean walk by the window and enter the shop. Alison does not see them come in. They walk up behind her. Gary, his hand in his pocket, sticks it in her back. We cannot tell if he is holding the gun or not.

Gary This is a stick up. Keep quiet and you won't get hurt. I want all the videos you've got in this sack.

Alison is terrified. Then she hears the boys laughing behind her and looks round. Her fear turns to anger.

Alison Fool! It's not funny!

Gary It was only a joke. We were just walking past.

Vic is grinning mischievously.

Vic He's got a present for you.

Gary looks at him angrily, but before Vic can continue teasing Gary about the perfume, Sean intervenes.

Sean Look at this Alison ...

He takes a tiny pair of headphones from around his neck and places them over Alison's ears ...

Alison What is it?

Sean plugs the lead into his wristwatch and presses a button on the watch.

Sean That's 'Radio Hallam'. You can get 'Radio 1' as well.

He is about to unplug the lead but Alison grabs his hand. She is listening intently then takes off the headphones. She is excited at something she's heard.

Alison They're having a pop quiz.

She pauses.

The winner gets a night out with Calvin Clark.

* *

Alison, Gary and Vic leave the video shop and crowd into a telephone box. Sean is standing outside. Throughout the scene, Sean keeps opening the door and popping his head into the box to listen to what is happening. The others, irritated by his persistence and trying to keep out the noise, keep pushing him out.

Gary is enjoying being crushed up against Alison in the telephone box. He is also jealous of the fact that Alison idolises Calvin Clark. A transistor radio, tuned to the local radio station, is standing on the shelf playing a pop record. The record ends and the D.J. speaks.

D.J. That was the fabulous Status Quo with their new single. And now for the next contestant in our Personality Pop Quiz. Our pop personality this week is Calvin Clark, the City and England star ... due to leave these shores to continue his career with the German club, Hamburg. Okay. Let's have our next contestant please ...

The telephone rings. Alison is so surprised that she does not pick it up immediately. Vic nudges her.

Vic Go on.

Alison picks up the telephone and speaks into it.

Alison Hello.

The D.J. replies and we hear the following telephone conversation.

D.J. Hello. Could I have your name please?

Alison Alison. Alison Connor.

D.J. And where do you live, Alison?

Alison Highfields.

D.J. And where do you work?

Alison I work in a video shop.

D.J. Can I ask how old you are?

Alison Yes. I'm eighteen.

D.J. Tell me Alison, are you a City supporter?

Alison Yeah. I go every week.

D.J. That's great. And what do you think about Calvin Clark going to Hamburg?

Alison Terrible. I'm heartbroken.

Gary looks sulky at this reply.

* *

Inside Calvin Clark's house. The lounge in the evening of day 3.

Calvin is throwing a farewell party for his City team mates. They are listening to the pop quiz on the radio. Most of them have cans of lager in their hands and their manner is loud and jocular. Calvin appears quite restrained compared to the others.

The players jeer and cheer at Alison's remark about being heartbroken.

Paul She'll be able to get some video nasties to take with you, Calvin! Killer Driller!

The D.J. speaks through the radio.

D.J. Okay, Alison. Here we go with our first question. Are you ready?

Alison replies over the radio.

Alison Yes.

The D.J. pauses.

D.J. On which London street was the Marquee first sited?

The players look puzzled.

Player I've never heard of it.

D.J. On which London street was the Marquee first sited?

One or two of the players make tentative suggestions but none of them know.

Alison Oxford Street.

D.J. Oxford Street! Correct! One down, two to go.

* *

Alison is looking pleased at getting the first answer correct. Sean has his head inside the box listening. We hear the phone conversation.

D.J. The second question is: Where is the legendary Jim Morrison of The Doors buried?

Alison, Gary and Vic glance at each other enquiringly. Sean giggles.

Sean In his coffin.

Angrily, Gary pushes him out of the telephone box.

Alison Can you repeat it, please?

Vic whispers the answer into Gary's ear. Gary nods and whispers it to Alison.

Paris.

D.J. Correct! Okay. This is getting really exciting now! One more correct answer Alison, and you win a fabulous night out at Millionaire's Night Club with Calvin Clark, England star and most expensive footballer in Britain! Isn't that something? I can hardly bear the tension.

He pauses.

Okay, Alison. Here we go. Question number three is: What do they call Mark E. Smith's wife?

Alison hasn't a clue. She hasn't known any of the answers. Vic and Gary are the pop experts. Vic furrows his brow in concentration. He doesn't know the answer. Gary gazes out through the door and appears disinterested.

Are you there, Alison?

Alison Yes, I'm just thinking ...

D.J. You've only got a few more seconds I'm afraid ...

Alison looks desperately from Gary to Vic. Gary is in an agony of indecision. If he tells Alison the answer, she will win a night out with Calvin Clark. On the other hand, it might put him in her good books. He relents and swiftly whispers the answer into Alison's ear.

Alison Brix!

D.J. Correct! And congratulations.

Alison leaps up and down in the limited space and hugs Gary who looks bashful at her embrace. Gary leans on the door and they all spill out onto the pavement.

* *

Inside Calvin Clark's house. The lounge in the evening of day 3.

The City players are teasing Calvin. They are delighted at the trick they have played on him. They set up the 'night out' without his knowledge and he only found out when they switched on the radio to listen to the quiz.

Paul You'll be all right there, Calvin. Nice little leaving present for you.

Player She might be a right bimbo.

The others laugh. Calvin shakes his head barely amused.

* *

Inside Alison's house. The bedroom in the evening of day 4.

Alison is gloomily examining her clothes in the wardrobe. She flicks the hangers along the rail, occasionally taking out a dress and holding it up before putting it back.

Paula (Sean and Gary's mother), dressed in a kissagram, Traffic Warden's uniform, is standing by the dressing table. Their friend, Sue, is sitting on the bed.

Sue Where are you working tonight?

Paula A Stag night at the Red Lion.

Alison I've nothing to wear, tomorrow night.

Paula You what! You've got more clothes than Lady Di.

Alison It's dead posh at Millionaire's you know. I want to look right.

Sue You're never satisfied. A free meal and a nice feller. What more do you want?

We hear the front door open. Gary speaks from the bottom of the stairs.

Gary Alison!

Paula sounds surprised.

Paula It's our Gary.

Alison I'm up here!

We hear Gary running up the stairs, then he enters the bedroom. He is holding a carrier bag. He is surprised and embarrassed to see his mother and Sue. He was expecting to see Alison on her own. Paula is grinning.

Paula This is what you get up to is it?

Sue I wish I'd a lad running up my stairs. I know that much.

Alison speaks to Gary.

Alison What do you want?

Gary pauses and looks embarrassed. He indicates the carrier bag.

Gary I've brought you something ... Anyway I'll ... . I'll come back later when you're on your own ... .

Sue snatches the bag from Gary's hand.

Sue Let's have a look then ...

She takes out a dress and holds it up.

Oh, isn't it lovely? It'll just fit me.

She stands in front of the wardrobe mirror and holds the dress up to herself. She is a large woman and the dress looks absurdly small against her. Alison and Paula laugh.

Paula Fit you! It wouldn't fit one of your legs!

Alison takes the dress from Sue and examines it. She holds it up to herself. We can tell she likes it.

It's nice. Black suits you.

Alison Where did you get it from?

Gary pauses.

Gary I bought it.
Alison Where from?
Gary A feller I know.
He pauses.
He gets them cheap.
Alison Are you sure? I'm not wearing it if it's nicked.
Gary It's not!
He pauses.
Honest.

* *

Outside Millionaire's Night Club. The evening of day 4.

Fashionably dressed young men and women are entering the club. Two bouncers on the door look them over to make sure they are up to standard.

A taxi pulls up outside the club. Alison gets out, pays the driver, then approaches the club. She speaks to the bouncers and one of them points inside. The bouncers turn and watch Alison go in to where Calvin is waiting.

* *

The Manager leads Alison and Calvin to their table. There is a background beat of dance music from the disco in the adjoining room. Alison looks very attractive. She is nervous but excited. She is in the smartest club in town with her hero. What more could she want? She notices people looking at them and nudging each other. She feels important. She feels like a star.

They reach a table with a 'reserved' card on it. The Manager pulls out a chair for Alison and she sits down.

Alison Thank you.

The Manager signals a waiter who arrives carrying a single red rose in a cellophane wrapper and a bottle of champagne in a wine cooler. He places the cooler on the table then hands the rose to Alison.

Manager For you, Madam.

Alison blushes.

Alison Thank you.

The waiter lifts the champagne out of the cooler and dries the bottle.

Waiter Good win today, Calvin. At least you're leaving on a high note.

Calvin Yeah. I suppose so.

Calvin glances round then smiles weakly at Alison. He looks dissatisfied. Alison seems a nice enough girl, and she is certainly attractive, but he would have preferred to have chosen his own partner on his last Saturday night out in the city.

The waiter opens the champagne, pours two glasses, then leaves the table. Calvin raises his glass.

Cheers.

They touch glasses.

Alison Cheers.

They sip the champagne approvingly.

Mmm. Nice and dry.

Calvin looks surprised.

Calvin Do you drink a lot of champagne then?

Alison My brother brings a bottle home sometimes. He never touches it, though. He only drinks lager.

* *

A City back street at night on day 4.

Gary, Vic and Sean are walking down a dark street keeping a sharp lookout as they try the doors of parked cars. Gary and Vic are drinking cans of lager. Sean is listening to his personal stereo.

Gary is in a foul mood, resentful of the fact that Calvin, rich and famous, is out with Alison at the best club in town, while he is out with a couple of kids in a mean, city backstreet.

Vic Alison looked great in that dress.

Gary does not reply.

I wish I was going with her.

He pauses.

Do you think he'll fancy her?

Gary How do I know?

Vic She fancies him. All the birds do. He can have any bird he wants.

Gary Yeah, 'cos he's famous that's all. They wouldn't want to know if he wasn't famous.

Vic Do you think she'd fancy me if I was famous?

Gary You! You've got no chance!

Gary takes his resentment out on Vic by launching into a spiteful, Kung-Fu, kick-fighting routine which, although appearing playful, is meant to hurt. Vic tries to make light of it, but in the end he has to defend himself and the fight looks like becoming serious.

Sean brings it to an end by finding an open car. He calls to them from across the road.

Sean Hey! There's one here!

Gary and Vic cross the road. When they reach the car, Gary kicks a tyre in disgust.

Gary There's no wonder. It's a Lada. Nobody's going to nick that, are they?

Gary slams the door and they continue down the street. Gary sees an ice-cream van.

Hey! Anyone fancy an ice-cream?

* *

Inside Millionaire's Night Club. The restaurant.

Alison and Calvin have started their meal. There is an uneasy silence between them. Calvin is virtually ignoring Alison. He keeps glancing across at a nearby table where a group of people are drunkenly celebrating a 21st birthday. He looks as if he would rather be with the party across the room than with Alison.

Calvin catches the eye of a young woman standing with a friend at the bar. She waves to Calvin then walks across to the table. She bends down and kisses Calvin on the cheek.

Zoe   Hello, Calvin, how are you?

Calvin   Zoe, where've you been? I haven't seen you for ages.

Zoe gives Alison a dismissive once-over then turns back to Calvin.

Zoe   I've been away. Working in London.

Calvin   Great!

Zoe   I hear you're going to Germany.

Calvin   Yeah. Next week.

Zoe   Give me a ring before you go.

Calvin   Yeah, I will.

Zoe   I'll see you then. Have a nice meal.

Calvin   See you later.

She returns to the bar. Calvin watches her go with a smile on his face. Alison feels even more rejected. There is a pause.

Alison Are you looking forward to going to Hamburg?

Calvin pauses.

Calvin I'm getting used to the idea.

Alison It's the biggest port in Germany. It's on the River Elbe.

Calvin looks surprised.

Calvin How do you know that?

Alison I looked it up.

Calvin smiles. It is the first time he has warmed to her all evening.

Two young women, giggling and slightly tipsy, detach themselves from the 21st birthday party across the room and approach the table.

Woman 1 Excuse me, can we have your autograph?

Calvin grins.

Calvin Sure.

The woman places her foot on the rung of Calvin's chair and rests a paper napkin on her thigh. Grinning, Calvin takes out a biro and signs his name. He repeats the process with the second woman.

Woman 2 Thanks.

As they return to their table, Alison notices Gary's mother, Paula, and the Manager enter the restaurant. The Manager points in their direction. Paula takes off her coat. She is dressed in a French maid's outfit with suspenders and stockings. She walks across the restaurant in the direction of Alison and Calvin's table. Calvin sees her coming.

Calvin Oh no!

But Paula passes their table and stops at the 21st birthday party. One of the guests points out the 'birthday boy' and Paula reads out a list of greetings from a giant birthday card then goes through her kissagram routine.

Paula finishes her performance. As she crosses the restaurant, she catches Alison's eye and tries to apologise with a resigned glance. Calvin looks amused.

I thought she was coming for me. I thought the lads had set me up again.

Alison What do you mean?

Calvin replies tactlessly.

Calvin Like they set me up for this: the City lads. They phoned Radio Hallam and put me down for the personality pop quiz. By the time I found out it was too late to back out. I'd got to come.

Alison feels deeply humiliated by this revelation.

I half expected some of them to appear and start jeering when I saw her walking over.

He laughs.

If it had been me though it'd have been a Boobagram.

He laughs again but Alison is not amused – her humiliation is giving way to anger.

They must be right slags to do that sort of thing.

Alison No, they're not!

Calvin looks surprised at her vehement response.

Calvin 'Course they are. Showing themselves off in public.

Alison You don't think she likes doing it. do you? She's doing it for the money, that's all. She's just trying to earn a living. We can't all earn thousands of pounds a week kicking a football around, you know.

She starts to get up. Calvin, realising how arrogant and insensitive he's been, takes her arm.

Wait.

He pauses

Calvin I'm sorry.

Alison glares at him,.

Honest.

Alison relaxes, then speaks with a flash of defiance.

Alison And don't think I'm going to ask you for your autograph, because I'm not.

They both laugh. The tension between them is broken.

* *

Inside an ice-cream van at night on day 4.

Gary, Vic and Sean are joyriding round the city in a stolen ice-cream van. Gary, wearing the vendor's white coat, is driving. Vic is sitting next to him eating an ice-cream and Sean is fiddling around with the dashboard. He sets off the musical chimes and for several seconds they travel to the accompaniment of 'Greensleeves'. Vic laughs. Gary is furious.

Gary Turn it off. Turn it off, you fool.

He switches off the chimes, clips Sean around the head and pushes him into the back of the van. They drive up to and park opposite the Millionaire's Club. Gary turns the engine off.

It is after midnight and people are leaving the club. Employees drive the customers' cars round to the front of the club from the car park.

Gary and Vic note the fashionably dressed men and women. Sean is more interested in licking every morsel off the wrapper of a choc-ice.

Vic If I was rich, I'd have a garage full of cars. I'd have a Lamborghini Contache ... a Ferrari Testarossa ... an Aston Martin ... a Lagonda ... .

A drunk appears and knocks on the window of the van.

Drunk Can I have a Cornetto?

Gary Sorry mate, we've none left.
Drunk What's that you're eating then?

Gary answers viciously.

Gary These are the last.

The drunk meanders off down the road.

Alison and Calvin leave the club. Calvin has his arm round Alison and they look happy together. Calvin's Porsche is driven round to the front of the club and Gary watches enviously as Calvin and Alison climb in and drive off.

Gary starts the ice-cream van and they follow the Porsche through the city streets. The Porsche pulls over onto a patch of quiet wasteland at the side of the canal. Gary stops the van and the boys watch from a distance. The Porsche is parked in a dark spot so the boys can only see shadowy figures inside the car.

Gary What do you think they're doing?
Vic I know what I'd be doing. Look! He's putting his arm round her!
Gary Is he heck! They're just talking.
Vic What into each other's mouths? He's kissing her, isn't he Sean?
Sean I can't tell. They look close though.
Gary You can't see. It's too dark.
Vic 'Course I can. I've got eyes like a hawk. I can see in the dark.

Gary can't stand any more. He drives the van onto the waste land and rams the back of the Porsche. After a shocked silence, Calvin scrambles out of the car and Gary, Vic and Sean get out of the van. Calvin is furious as he inspects the car. He takes no notice of Alison who is still inside.

Calvin You stupid ... Look what you've done! It's ruined!
Gary Never mind that. What were you doing in there with her?

Calvin	What you talking about? Anyway what's it to you what I was doing? It's none of your business!
	Alison gets out of the car, shaken, not sure what is happening. But she soon comes to her senses when she sees the three lads.
Alison	You lot! What the hell do you think you're doing?
	Calvin looks amazed.
Calvin	Do you know them?
Alison	Know them! I wish I didn't!
	Sean peers at the dashboard of the damaged Porsche.
Sean	It does 165 m.p.h. Vic!
Calvin	Get away from it!
	Gary speaks to Alison.
Gary	Slag! You've only been with him ten minutes and he's getting his leg over!
Calvin	Hey! Who do you think you're calling a slag?
	Calvin throws a punch at Gary and knocks him to the ground. Gary is humiliated, flattened in front of Alison, his brother and his mate. Sean runs at Calvin, arms flailing, and tries to head butt him in the stomach. Calvin pushes him away contemptuously. Gary gets up. He looks dangerous. He attacks Calvin with a series of high kicks and kicks him in the face. Calvin staggers, his hands over his face. Sean, still furious at Gary's knock-down and being treated contemptuously by Calvin, snatches up a half-brick and throws it at Calvin. Calvin goes down immediately. He lies still. There is a shocked silence.
Alison	You've killed him! He's dead!
	She tries to revive him. Sean starts to cry. He is suddenly a frightened little boy. Alison puts her ear to Calvin's mouth and chest.
	He's breathing! He's still alive!
Vic	What we going to do now?
Gary	Leave him. Come on. Let's go!

Alison You can't do that. It's serious. He might die.

Sean is still snivelling, still frightened at what he has done.

We'll have to take him to hospital.

Gary No way! Come on, let's go.

Vic Yeah, but what about when he comes round and the police turn up? He's seen us hasn't he?

Gary looks around. He is in a panic. Things are getting out of control. He just wants to get away.

Gary Put him in the van.

Alison What for? Where you taking him?

Gary shouts.

Gary I don't know! Just get him in the van!

The boys carry and drag the unconscious Calvin to the van and bundle him inside. Gary speaks to Vic.

Tie him up.

Then he speaks to Sean.

You come with me.

Vic and Alison climb into the van. Gary and Sean walk across to the Porsche. Gary opens the door and releases the handbrake.

Sean What you doing?

Gary Come on. Push …

They push the car, then leave it to accelerate down the slope into the canal. They watch it sink, then run back to the ice-cream van, jump in and drive off.

Vic is sitting with Gary in the front of the van. Alison and Sean are in the back with Calvin, who is lying on the floor unconscious with his hands and feet tied.

Alison is beside herself. It's like a bad dream! She can't believe what's happening to her! Sean is still terrified at what he has done to Calvin. What if he dies?

Alison	Take him to the hospital Gary. He looks bad.
Gary	He'll be all right in a bit.
Alison	What if he's in a coma? What if he doesn't come round?
Gary	We can't take him to hospital.
Alison	Why can't you?
Gary	Because he'll tell on us, won't he stupid? He'll have us put away!
Alison	You want putting away! In a mental hospital! The lot of you!

Calvin starts to moan. His eyelids flutter.

Alison	He's coming round! He's going to be all right.

Gary produces the gun from his pocket and passes it to Vic. Alison flips when she sees the gun.

Oh my God, where you got that from? Put it away! For God's sake put it away!

Gary	Cover him!
Vic	Cover him? What for?
Gary	In case he gets away.
Vic	No chance! Houdini couldn't get out of that.

Calvin opens his eyes and groans.

Gary	Gag him! For Christ's sake shut him up.

Vic looks round for something to gag him with, then produces a snotty, screwed up handkerchief from his pocket and opens it out.

Alison	You're not using that! What you trying to do now, kill him with germ warfare.

Sean opens the refrigerator and takes out an ice lolly. He removes the paper then gently rubs the ice lolly up and down Calvin's cheek which is swollen from Gary's kick.

What do you think you're doing, stupid?

Sean speaks with no sense of irony.

Sean It's to stop his eye going black.

Alison starts to cry. She can't cope with it. She's had enough and shouts at Gary.

Alison Where we going anyway? Where you taking us?

Gary does not reply. They drive on.

* *

The van drives up to the derelict council flats.

Gary and Vic are directing Alison and Calvin along the walkway of the top floor of the flats.

They stop at one of the flats. Vic opens the door and they push Alison and Calvin inside.

Calvin's hands are tied and he is still gagged. Vic lights two candles. Gary shoves Calvin roughly onto the mattress on the floor. Alison looks around.

Alison God what a dump. What you brought us here for?

Vic points to Calvin.

Vic What we going to do with him?

Gary does not know. They have been driven to the flat by circumstance rather than logic. They have reached the end of the line. Then Gary has a brainwave.

Gary We're holding him to ransom.

Vic and Sean look as surprised as Alison and Calvin.

Alison You're what? No, Gary. You must be mad!

Gary Why not? We've nothing to lose. We can't let him go now or he'll turn us in. We might as well make the best of it and make some money out of him while we can.

He pauses.

Anyway, if Hamburg can afford three million for him, they can afford half a million for us.

Alison speaks indignantly.

Alison You can't keep him here! He's not fit! He needs a doctor!

Alison buttons up Calvin's ripped shirt.

He'll freeze to death. It's like a fridge in here.

She fusses over Calvin, wiping his bloodied face while Gary looks on jealously. Gary can't stand anymore and pulls her away.

Gary Get away from him!

Alison is angry and close to tears.

Alison And what about me? Are you holding me to ransom too?

The boys glance at each other. They are not sure what to do with her.

Vic You'll have to stay here 'til it's over.

Alison And what about my mother? What do you think she's going to do when I don't come home?

They pause. They hadn't thought of that.

She'll go to the police won't she?

Gary Okay. You can go. And keep your mouth shut! And take our Sean with you.

Sean I'm not! I'm staying here!

Gary No, you're not. You're going home.

Sean I'm not! I'll tell my mum! I'll tell the police!

Gary I'll smack you in the gob if you don't shut it!

Vic Let him stay. He'll be all right. He'll be safer here anyway where we can keep an eye on him.

Gary concedes reluctantly.

Gary Yeah. I suppose so.

Alison And how am I supposed to get home?

Gary speaks to Vic.

Gary I'll give her a lift in the van and then get rid of it. It's not safe on the streets at this time of night. Too many nutters about.

Alison speaks to Calvin.

Alison God I feel terrible leaving you like this. I feel it's all my fault. I'll come and see you again.

Then defiantly to the boys.

And don't lay another finger on him or you'll be in worse trouble. Right!

Gary pushes her out of the room.

Gary Come on ...

As he closes the door, Vic and Sean call after him.

Vic Get some crisps!

Sean And some pop.

* *

Alison and Gary are leaving the flat, walking towards the ice-cream van.

Alison is angry and frightened. Gary is embarrassed. He doesn't know what to say to her now that they are on their own. There is a pause.

Gary Did you have a nice time tonight?

Alison Yeah. Great! Terrific! The best night out I've ever had!

She pauses.

Let him go, Gary, before it's too late. He'll not tell if you let him go now.

Gary No way.

Alison You'll go to prison, you know that don't you?

Gary Will you come and see me?

Alison Oh yes. Definitely. I'll buy a season ticket for Dartmoor.

Gary We're not going to prison. We're going to be rich.

Shooting Stars

He pauses.

We're helping ourselves like the Government says.

* *

Outside Sean and Gary's house at night.

Sean and Gary's mum, Paula, wearing her coat over her French maid's outfit is standing on the doorstep peering up and down the street. She looks at her watch. It is 2.30 a.m. She hears footsteps and Alison approaches.

Alison What you doing?

Paula I'm looking for our Sean. Look at the time Alison. I'm worried sick.

Alison It's all right. I've seen him. He's with your Gary. They're stopping at Robert Mitchell's.

Paula They never said anything to me.

Alison I saw them in town. They asked me to tell you.

She indicates Paula's open coat which is revealing her French maid's outfit.

I'd go in if I was you or you'll catch cold.

Paula pulls her coat to.

Paula I'm sorry about tonight. Did I embarrass you? It was a last minute booking.

Alison It's all right. I must admit I was a bit worried though when I saw you coming towards our table.

Paula How did you get on?

Alison All right.

Paula Is he nice?

Alison Yeah, lovely.

Paula Are you going to see him again?

Alison speaks with no trace of irony.

Alison I hope so. He's a bit tied up this week though. See you.

She continues down the street. Paula gives one last look up and down the street then goes inside.

* *

A City back street on day 5.

Gary is approaching a telephone box. He goes inside, takes out a scrap of paper with the City number on it and dials ... He speaks into the phone with an Irish accent.

Gary I want to speak to the Manager. It's urgent. It's about Calvin Clark.

(*He pauses – Gary slips some more coins in the box.*)

Hello ... . Yes. Listen. We've got Calvin Clark. We're holding him to ransom ... . No, it not a hoax. It's deadly serious ... . And listen. Don't phone the police or you'll never see him again. All right? Now this is what we want ... . We want a half a million pounds. You heard right. A half a million ... Bring it to the Bus Station. Platform 'B'. I'll be in touch ...

* *

Inside the derelict flat on day 5.

Calvin, his ankles tied together with a bike lock, is sitting on the sofa eating a bag of crisps. Sean is sitting next to him asking him jokes from a joke book.

Gary, lounging on the mattress, and Vic, sitting on a chair, are also eating snacks. Sean watches Calvin eat his crisps.

Sean What's your favourite flavour?

Calvin does not reply.

Mine's smoky bacon. Do you like twiglets?

Calvin ignores him and addresses Gary and Vic.

Calvin Do you think they're going to let you get away with half a million quid?

Vic and Gary do not reply.

They'll have told the police by now. They'll be looking all over for me.

Gary You've nothing to worry about then, have you? You'll be home in time to watch 'Neighbours' at tea time.

Sean Why did the hedgehog cross the road?

Calvin doesn't know. He doesn't care. He is exhausted and irritable after a sleepless night.

To see his flat mate.

Sean pauses.

You can get hedgehog flavoured crisps now.

He turns a page.

What do you call a gorilla with bananas in its ear.

Calvin turns angrily on Sean.

Calvin Look, shut your face, will you!

Gary and Vic laugh.

Sean How much do you get paid?

Calvin Mind your own business.

Gary speaks bitterly.

Gary I'll tell you how much I get: £27.40 a week.

Calvin pauses, then speaks vindictively.

Calvin I'll be on five grand a week at Hamburg plus a fifty thousand signing on fee. Then there's win bonuses, points bonuses, sponsorship deals, a house, a car ... .

There is an awed silence as the boys take this in.

Sean I'm going to be a footballer.

Gary Wait till we get the ransom money though.

* *

The City stadium on day 5.

Karl Gutke, the Hamburg F.C. Manager, is in conversation with Southgate and Price.

The three men walk along the top tier of the deserted stand, with the players training far below them on the pitch.

Southgate It might be university students. A charity stunt, something like that. You know what they're like. You can't move these days without somebody rattling a tin in your face.

Price He didn't sound like a university student. He was Irish. Sounded like Terry Wogan.

Gutke We have to take this seriously. Half a million pounds is a lot of money. Maybe it is the IRA.

Price I think we should get the police in, let them sort it out.

Gutke I am not too sure. If the police are involved they will mount a big operation which could endanger Calvin's life.

Price He's got a point there. You know what they're like. He could end up on the physio's table being treated for bullet wounds.

He pauses.

Or worse.

Southgate	So, what do you suggest we do?
Gutke	Pay them.
	Southgate and Price look at him in surprise.
	I don't care about the money. I want Calvin safe. I want him at Hamburg.
Southgate	But what if they don't release him when they've got the money?
Gutke	That is a risk we shall have to take. It is dangerous either way.
	Southgate pauses.
Southgate	Well it's up to you in the end. He's your player.
Gutke	No. Not yet he isn't.
Southgate	What do you mean? He signed when he went over for his medical last week.
	Gutke shakes his head.
Gutke	No. We are still waiting for the full report. It is only a formality, but legally he is still a City player. So what do you want to do?
	Southgate considers the options.
Southgate	Mm. A dead striker's not going to do my cash flow problem much good, is he?
	Gutke walks away from the other two men. Realising the implications of this, Southgate turns furiously on Price.
	Why the hell didn't you tell me?
Price	How did I know? He never said anything when he came back. I thought it was all settled.

* *

A city back street on day 5.
Paula, wearing her nurse's kissagram outfit under her

coat, is walking down a street of terraced houses. She stops at one of the houses and knocks on the door. A dishevelled youth in T-shirt and jeans opens the door.

Robert   Hello, Mrs Gibson. I thought it was the social worker.

Paula   Are our Gary and Sean here?

Robert looks puzzled and shakes his head.

Robert   No. Why?

Paula   They didn't stop here last night, then?

Robert looks bemused.

Robert   No. What would they want to stop here for?

Paula walks away without answering him. Robert looks after her, then shakes his head in bewilderment and goes back inside. Paula walks on. She sees Alison and runs to catch up with her.

Paula   Alison!

Alison pretends not to hear and quickens her pace.

Alison!

Alison has to look round now. Paula catches her up.

Have you seen our Gary and Sean?

Alison feigns surprise.

Alison   No. Aren't they back yet?

Paula pauses.

Paula   Alison. I've been round to Robert Mitchell's.

Alison averts her eyes and does not answer. Paula loses her temper with her.

Listen, Alison! I've had enough. I want to know what's going on! I want to know where they are!

Paula grabs hold of her.

If you don't tell me, I'm going to the police.

Alison shakes her head wildly.

Alison   You can't!

Paula   Why can't I? What have they done?

Alison still refuses to answer.

Right! That's it! If they're in trouble that's their fault! The police can sort it out!

Alison can see that she is worried enough to carry out her threat. She pauses.

Alison They've kidnapped Calvin Clark. They're holding him to ransom.

Paula gapes at her, dumbstruck.

Paula They've what?

Alison When we were driving back from Millionaire's, they ran into us, Gary, Sean and Vic, in a van. They took him off and said they were going to ask for a ransom from City.

Paula Good God! Where've they taken him.

Alison pauses.

Alison I don't know. They took me to Stanley Square then I took a taxi home.

Paula They must be mad. They'll get life if they're caught.

She starts to cry.

Our Sean. Our little Sean. At least they could have sent him home.

She cries into her hands. Tony, who has come to take Paula to work, draws up in his car across the road and sounds his horn. Paula takes her compact out of her handbag and looks at herself in the mirror.

Oh my God! Look at the state of me! They'll want their money back.

She hurriedly applies lipstick and dabs the runny mascara underneath her eyes.

Look at my eyes …

Alison They'll not be looking at your eyes.

Paula is forced to laugh in spite of everything.

Paula Don't be awful, Alison!

She runs across the road, gets into the car and Tony drives off.

* *

Inside the derelict flat at night on day 5.

Gary and Vic are playing cards on the mattress. Calvin, sitting on the sofa with his ankles tied, is throwing the plastic football for Sean to head back to him.

Calvin ... That's it. Use your forehead not the top of your head.

Calvin is having difficulty catching the ball because of Sean's inaccurate returns. Sean unfastens the bike lock around his ankles. Gary notices what is happening.

Gary What you doing?

Sean He can't catch it properly.

Gary turns back to the game of cards.

Vic Do you think they'll get half a million pounds into a sportsbag?

Gary Dunno ...

He picks up the full pack of cards.

Say that's fifty, fifty pound notes.

He works it out on his calculator.

That's two thousand five hundred pounds.

Vic Yeah, but a card's thicker than a note, isn't it?

Gary ignores him and makes a second calculation.

Gary That's two hundred bundles.

Across the room, Calvin keeps one eye on Gary and Vic as he teaches Sean how to head the football.

Calvin	That's it. Use your forehead … Keep your eyes open … Get your arms out. Nice and balanced …
Vic	Perhaps we should ring up, tell them to put it in something bigger.
Gary	Yeah, why not? I'll tell them to put it in a Pickford's van and ask them to deliver.

Suddenly, Calvin makes a dash for the door. With lightning reactions, Vic dives across the floor and trips him up. They roll around the floor struggling violently. Gary pulls out the gun and points it at them, trying to isolate Calvin.

Get off him! Let him go! Let him go or I'll kill you …!

Gary works himself up into a frenzy. He can't get a clear aim at Calvin. Finally, in a fit of frustration he pulls the trigger and fires into the wall above them. The shot is deafening in the confines of the small room and terrifies all of them. Vic, Calvin and Sean curl up on the floor, their arms round their heads, wondering what has happened.

* *

Alison, carrying a shoulder bag, is walking along the balcony towards the flat. She hears the gun shot, pauses, then starts to run.

* *

Vic is getting to his feet. Calvin is lying on the floor. Gary is still holding the gun. There is a frantic banging on the door. The boys jump and look at each other. Gary pauses.

Gary	Who is it?
Alison	It's me! Let me in!
	Vic opens the door. Alison pushes past him and sees Calvin on the floor, the gun in Gary's hand ...
Alison	Oh my God!
	She bends down beside Calvin.
	Calvin! Are you all right?
Calvin	Yeah ...
	Realising that he hasn't been shot, Alison weeps with relief. Sean speaks excitedly.
Sean	Alison! Calvin tried to escape and our Gary fired a shot! Look! It hit the wall.
	Alison turns on Gary angrily.
Alison	You nutter! You could have killed him!
Gary	It was his own fault! He shouldn't have tried to escape!
Alison	When I heard that shot I was terrified.
Calvin	You're not the only one.
	Alison opens her shoulder bag.
Alison	I've brought you a few things ...
	She takes out one of her sweaters.
	This'll keep you warm ...
	It's a bit tight but it'll keep you warm.
	(*She helps Calvin to pull it on.*)
	She pulls at it in places then smoothes her hand down the front.
Calvin	Yeah .... Thanks .... Great ...
	Alison takes a flask out of her bag and unscrews the cap.
Alison	I've brought you some soup ....
	She holds the cup to his mouth and he has a drink. The boys watch enviously.
	I bet you're starving aren't you?
Gary	He's had as much food as us. We've shared it out.

Shooting Stars

Sean Can I have a drink, Alison?

Alison You! I wouldn't give you a drink of rat poison!
She turns back to Calvin and gently strokes his cheek.
How's your eye?

Calvin It's all right. At least I can see through it now.

Alison I feel terrible. I feel as if it's all my fault.

Calvin Why should you? You're not to blame.

Alison I know. But if I hadn't won the pop quiz and that none of this would have happened, would it?

Calvin You weren't to know were you? You can't blame yourself for what they did.

Alison You must think I'm awful knowing this load of no hopers.
She indicates the three boys. Gary is furious.

Gary Just watch who you're calling a no hoper, will you?

Alison What do you expect me to call you, keeping him here like this? A hero?

Gary Just wait 'til we get the ransom money and we're rich. You'll be singing a different song then.

Alison And when's that going to be?

Gary When I arrange the pick up.

Alison I wouldn't touch that money with a barge pole.

Sean I'm going to give my share to my mum so she can give up work and stop at home.

* *

Inside the derelict flat on day 6.

Vic is spraying graffiti on the walls from a paint can. Calvin lying on the sofa with his arms and legs tied, watches him sullenly, Sean is sitting on the mattress listening to his personal stereo and reading his joke book.

Vic's paint runs out. He throws the can on the floor.

Vic Get me some more paint when you go out, Sean.

Calvin speaks to Vic.

Calvin You got a job?

Vic pauses.

Vic Yeah. I work in a restaurant.

Calvin Won't you get the sack?

Vic Who cares? Who wants to wipe tables in a paper hat?

He pauses.

Do you know what I did before that?

He pauses.

I worked in a cake factory making jam rolls. Before that, a barber's sweeping up and making tea. I never got near the scissors.

He pauses.

You know at Millionaire's when them guys parked your car for you? I did that as well. Grinning my face off and hoping for a big tip.

Calvin Is that why you did it, cos you were jealous?

Vic looks round at him scornfully.

Vic Wouldn't you be fucking jealous if it was the other way round?

Calvin Hey, I wasn't brought up in Buckingham Palace you know. I lived in a flat like this. I worked in a sausage factory when I left school.

Vic So what? What are you trying to say? Just because we're both black don't mean we've got anything in common you know. It's rich and poor that counts, not black and white. When I drove them cars round the front of Millionaire's, there were as many black bastards as white bastards I can tell you.

Calvin replies angrily.

Calvin Okay. But let me tell you something. When a guy on the other team calls you a black bastard to wind you up; or somebody in the crowd throws a banana on the pitch and makes monkey noises, it don't matter if you're on ten grand a week or ten quid, it hurts! All the money in the world don't protect you from that!

Calvin glares at Vic, challenging him to refute it. Sean takes off his earphones and reads out a joke from his book.

Sean What did the woman say when her photographs were late?

Pause.

Some day my prints will come.

Vic and Calvin are barely listening. Sean frowns at the book.

I don't get it.

Calvin tries to make Sean shut up.

Calvin It's a song.

Sean What is?

There is a knock on the door.

Gary It's only me.

Sean runs over and unlocks the door. Gary walks in.

Gary Okay. It's fixed. They've got the money.

Vic Great.

Sean looks at his joke book.

Sean Gary, do you know a song called, 'Some day my prints will come'?

Gary scowls at him.

Gary What you on about?

Vic and Calvin exchange amused glances in spite of their mutual antipathy.

* *

Outside the Carlton Hotel at night on day 6.

The Carlton is the most expensive hotel in the city. Paula gets off a bus outside the hotel and goes inside.

She approaches the Reception Desk. She is dressed up and looks very attractive.

Paula Excuse me, is Karl Gutke staying here?

Receptionist Mr Gutke? Yes. He's just gone through to the restaurant.

Paula Thank you.

Paula crosses the foyer and enters the restaurant.

Gutke is sitting at a table reading a German newspaper. Paula stands at the door, spots him, then walks across to his table. She pauses.

Paula Excuse me, Mr Gutke.

Gutke looks over his paper, surprised.

Gutke Yes?

Paula Could I have a word with you please?

Gutke pauses.

Gutke Certainly.

He pauses.

Would you like to sit down?

Paula Thank you.

Paula sits down.

Gutke Would you like a drink?

Paula Yes please. I'll have a gin and tonic.

Gutke catches a waiter's eye and orders.

I haven't been here before. It's nice.

Gutke It is the same as hotels all over the world.

Paula I wouldn't know. I've never stayed in one.

The waiter arrives with Paula's drink.

Waiter Shall I put it on your bill, sir?

Gutke Yes, please.

Shooting Stars

The waiter walks away.

Paula Cheers.

They raise their glasses and drink. Paula puts down her glass, opens her handbag and takes out a yellowing newspaper photograph. She hands it to Gutke who laughs in astonishment.

Gutke It is the 1966 World Cup team!

Paula leans across and points to one of the players.

Paula That's you isn't it?

Gutke Yes. That's me. I had more hair then.

He laughs.

Where did you get this?

Paula It's from my dad's scrapbook. He gave it to me before he died.

Gutke smiles at the photograph.

Gutke The third goal by England in the final did not go in you know. I have studied the film many times and I am convinced the ball did not cross the line.

He pauses.

Still, that is all a long time ago now. I have more important things to think about.

He hands back the photograph. Paula replaces it in her bag.

Paula That's why I came to see you.

She pauses.

I know about Calvin Clark. I know that he's been kidnapped and I might be able to help you find him.

Gutke looks astonished.

Gutke How do you know this?

Paula It doesn't matter. But I think I know who's done it.

Gutke You do! Who are they?

Paula I can't tell you their names. But if we could find them, they might listen to you and let him go.

Gutke I do not think so. We are dealing with ruthless criminals. We think the I.R.A. are involved.

Paula I.R.A.! Them three ... !

She stops herself in time.

Gutke Which three?

Paula Nothing. Listen.

She takes his arm.

I can't tell you anymore. You'll just have to trust me.

Gutke shakes his head.

Gutke It is too dangerous.

Paula Please ...

Gutke But why?

Paula Because I know them.

She pauses.

And because I don't want anything to happen to Calvin. We're proud of him round here you know. When he plays for England, it's as if he's playing for us, the people of this city. People who've never heard of Hamburg will be looking at the German results now to see how you've got on, and to see if Calvin's scored.

Paula expects Gutke to be grateful for her offer to help him. She is sadly mistaken. Gutke pauses.

Gutke I must be frank with you. These men have committed a criminal act. What they have done is wicked and immoral. They have put an innocent man's life at risk. If you do know anything, you should tell me or you could find yourself implicated in this crime.

Paula I'm just trying to help that's all.

Gutke You could help by telling me what you know.

Paula I have done!

Gutke I do not think so.

Paula In that case there's no point in me stopping, is there?

Shooting Stars

She finishes her drink and stands up ready to leave.

Gutke Where are you going now?

Paula I'm going home.

Gutke I'll give you a lift.

Paula It's all right. I'll get a bus.

Gutke It is no problem. I have a car.

Paula Honestly. I can get a taxi.

Gutke I insist.

Paula realises that her protests are futile. Gutke is determined to take her home, but this is the last thing she wants. Once Gutke knows where she lives, he will be able to make enquiries about her family. He might find out that Gary and Sean are missing.

Paula and Gutke leave the bar together.

* *

Inside Gutke's car at night on day 6.

Gutke is driving Paula home. They are passing through a rough area of tough pubs and seedy clubs. Paula is desperately wondering how she can get away from Gutke.

Paula Will you stop a minute? I want some fags.

Gutke stops the car. Paula opens the door.

I'll not be a minute.

Gutke I'll come with you.

Paula glances at him. She knows that he knows what she is up to. They get out of the car and enter the pub. Paula is slipping coins into a cigarette machine. Gutke looks around apprehensively. The room is full of dodgy-looking customers. Gutke does not feel at home here. Paula does. She offers him a cigarette. Gutke shakes his head.

Paula	Would you like a drink?
Gutke	No, thank you. I would like to go now.
Paula	Excuse me. I'll just go to the ladies …

Gutke watches her suspiciously as she walks away. What is she up to now? Paula stops and speaks to a boy playing a fruit machine. She asks him if he has seen Gary and Sean. He keeps his eyes on the machine as he shakes his head.

Paula enters the ladies. Gutke feels helpless. His eyes are fixed on the lavatory door. He realises that Paula has tricked him and that she is not going to come out. He hurries from the pub …

* *

Outside a public house at night on day 6.

Outside the pub, Gutke sees that his car has been vandalised. The front wheels have been removed and the car jacked up on two beer crates. Gutke is furious. He looks around and glimpses Paula running away in the distance. She turns a corner. Gutke chases her and stops her. Paula angrily shakes him off. They are both out of breath.

Paula	Let go of me! You're worse than the police!
Gutke	Why are you running away from me?
Paula	Cos you're bugging me that's why! Just go away, will you, and leave me alone!

Paula walks away angrily. Gutke follows her, chastened by her rebuke.

Gutke	My car has been victimised.
Paula	I know the feeling.
Gutke	The wheels have been stolen. I will have to find a phone box and ring a taxi.

Paula You've about as much chance of finding a phone that works round here as you have a job. Come on, and we'll make a few enquiries about Calvin on the way.

They set off down the road …

* *

Paula and Gutke approach the Truckers' Club which is situated next to the truck stop. The bouncer on the door is Robert Mitchell. He grins when he sees Paula.

Robert Hello Mrs Gibson. Found your Gary yet?

Paula glances uneasily at Gutke.

Paula Yeah. He'd been at an all night party. He was still bevied when he got home.

She pauses.

Can we use the phone Robert? Mr Gutke's car's been vandalised and he wants to phone a cab.

Robert Yeah. 'Course you can.

Paula and Gutke enter the club.

* *

Inside the Trucker's Club at night on day 6.

Paula and Gutke walk across the club. They reach the telephone. Gutke takes out a card with a taxi service on it and dials. He orders a cab then turns round. Paula has disappeared. He looks round then leaves the club. Standing outside the door, he looks round for Paula but she has disappeared into the night.

* *

Inside the City Football Club. The boardroom on day 7.

Southgate, Price and Gutke are filling a City sportsbag with wads of notes. They stuff in the last wad and Southgate zips up the bag. They get into Price's car and drive towards the bus station. They park where they can see the pick-up spot in the Bus Station.

Southgate is sitting next to Price. Gutke is in the back of the car. Price glances at his watch.

Price Have I to take it?

Gutke No, I'll go. Somebody might recognise you.

Gutke gets out of the car and picks up the sports bag containing the ransom money, off the back seat. He crosses the road to the bus station, walks along Platform 'B', then sits down on a bench with the bag at his feet. The Bus Station is busy and buses are arriving and leaving all the time.

A man sits down on the bench and starts to read a newspaper. Gutke glances at him. Is this the pick-up man? Gutke slides the bag under bench, waits a few moments, then stands up and returns to the car.

* *

Price, Southgate and Gutke are sitting in the car watching the bench. They can see the sports bag under the seat. The man reading the newspaper is still sitting there.

Price Do you reckon he's one of them?

Southgate He doesn't look very dangerous if he is.

Price I suppose you could say that about Hitler.

Then he apologises to Gutke.

Sorry about that, Karl.

The bus arrives. The man reading the paper stands up and gets on it.

Southgate	It's not him then.
Price	Perhaps they've bottled it.

Two girls, about 10–11 years old, walk up to the bench. One of them notices the bag, looks round, then pulls it out from under the bench. The girls say something to each other, glance round, then walk away with the bag. They are quickly lost in the crowd.

Bloody hell! Fancy using kids.

Gutke	They are very clever. They do not want to reveal themselves.
Southgate	What if we'd informed the police and there'd been a shoot-out?

He pauses.

They must be absolutely ruthless.

The others nod solemnly at the thought of it.

* *

Gary runs towards the Bus Station. He is late for the pick-up. He slows down. He is exhausted and out of breath. He makes his way across the Bus Station. He stops at the end of Platform 'B', looks round, then walks towards the pick-up bench. There is nobody sitting on it and nothing underneath it. Gary glances round in panic. They've double-crossed him! They've told the police! Suddenly everybody is a threat: the man standing at the bus stop, the two men talking together. He is convinced that he is surrounded. He walks away quickly then starts to run. As he dashes across the road, we can see that Price's car has already left.

* *

Inside the Bus Station. The Lost Property Office on day 7.

The two girls carry the sports bag to the counter and lift it on.

Girl 1 We've found this.

Attendant Right. Let's see if there's an address inside, shall we?

She unzips the bag and sees the wads of notes.

Good Lord!

She takes out a few wads and places them on the counter. The girls stare at them, wide-eyed. People gather round, excited.

Where did you find this?

Girl 2 Under a bench.

Attendant I think we'd better phone the police.

She picks up a telephone on the counter and dials. The second girl stares at the notes.

Girl 2 Will there be a reward?

The first girl turns to her angrily.

Girl 1 You stupid cow!

* *

Inside the City Football Club. The manager's office on day 7.

Price, Southgate and Gutke are nervously waiting to hear from the 'international' gang of kidnappers.

Southgate I hope we've done the right thing.

Price We've kept our side of the bargain. Let's hope they keep theirs.

Price opens a drawer in his filing cabinet and takes out a gallon bottle of whisky and three glasses. Gutke looks at the enormous bottle in amazement.

Gutke You must be under a lot of strain in your job.

Price laughs.

Price I was Bell's Whisky Manager of the Month in October. This was my prize.

Gutke It will last a long time.

Price pours the drinks.

Price It won't if this business goes on much longer.

The telephone rings. Southgate picks it up immediately and speaks.

Southgate Okay. Put him through ... Yes, speaking ... What do you mean? We did bring it. Left it under the bench as arranged. Half past two on the dot ... What about the girls then, what did they do with the stuff? ...

He is starting to get angry.

Don't give me that! You know very well what I mean! What are you trying to do, double-cross us? Isn't half a million enough? ... Don't you call me a liar! The money was there, as arranged ...! How the hell do I know who they were? We thought you'd sent them to pick it up ... You what? No way! No way! We kept our side of the bargain ... don't you threaten me! And listen, if anything happens to Clark, you'll be in worse trouble than you are now!

He slams down the phone.

Gutke What did he say?

Southgate He says he knows nothing about the kids picking the money up. He thinks we've reneged.

Gutke Do you believe what he says?

Southgate I don't know what to believe.

Price What about the money then? Who's got that if he's telling the truth?

Southgate God knows. But we've got to get it back.

* *

Inside the derelict flat at night on day 7.

Gary, Vic and Sean are huddled together reading the main story on the front of the local evening paper. The headline reads: Mystery Cash Haul Found! Gary and Vic are furious. Calvin watches them apprehensively from the sofa. How is this turn of events going to affect him?

Gary That was our money.

Vic Yeah, if you'd got there on time.

Gary How was I to know there'd be a traffic jam?

Vic What you talking about? There are traffic jams all the time. They're not new, man!

He walks away angrily.

Half a million quid just sitting there and you're late for the pick-up.

Gary Okay. Why didn't you go then?

Vic Cos you took control! Like you always do! Big man! We'd have been out of here by now!

Gary pauses.

Gary Okay. So nothing's changed. We've still got him. We can still get the money.

Vic Oh, yeah! Make sure you arrange it for midnight next time, when the streets are empty.

Sean We could cut one of his fingers off. Or a toe like they did in 'Death Dealers', to show them we mean business.

Gary clips Seans round the ear.

Gary He wouldn't be much use without his toes, would he? He wouldn't be worth two pence then.

He lashes the plastic football at Calvin in frustration. Sean picks up one of Vic's paint cans and sprays goal posts on opposite walls. Gary and Vic are too angry and fed up to take any notice of him.

Sean Do you want a game, Calvin?

Calvin shakes his head. Gary turns on him viciously.

Gary Why not, do you think you're too good for us or something?

Calvin does not answer.

Yes you do. Just cos you wear flash suits and drive a flash car, you think you're big. You think you're somebody.

Again, Calvin does not respond.

You think we're nobodies, don't you?

Calvin stares at him scornfully.

Calvin You said it.

Gary is working himself up into a frenzy.

Gary Well, we're not see! And you can have all the suits, and all the cars and all the money in the world, but you're still a black bastard!

Vic Hey! Watch it man!

Gary rounds on Vic.

Gary What's the matter with you? You on his side or something?

Vic No, but just watch your mouth!

Gary I'm not talking to you! You're different. You're one of us.

Vic Okay. But watch it!

There is a tense silence in the room which is eventually broken by Sean.

Sean Play Calvin, or the sides won't be equal.

Calvin pauses, hoping for another chance to escape.

Calvin Okay. At least it'll get the blood moving.

Sean unties Calvin and he stands up, stretching and flexing his legs.

What is it then, Black vs White?

Vic swiftly defuses the situation.

Vic Me and Gary'll take you and Sean.

Sean Wait till I tell my friends at school that I've played with Calvin Clark.

Gary You'd better not you fool, or you'll finish up in D.C.

They kick the rubbish to the side of the room and remove the sofa, mattress and chairs to the next room.

They kick off. It is a rough and hectic game with the ball ricochetting off the walls. It is obvious that Gary is out to get Calvin, but Calvin is used to being a marked man. He is quick and skilful and usually manages to shoot, or pass the ball to Sean before Gary can get near him. When Gary does get a tackle in, he tries to hurt Calvin, but Calvin takes his rough treatment without complaint. He is biding his time, waiting for an opportunity to get his own back.

Sean keeps the score. They argue heatedly over disputed goals, conceding some, insisting on others. Calvin is no longer a three million pound international, he is a youth again, enjoying the hurly-burly of a kick-about with his mates. Calvin flicks the ball up with his foot and starts to juggle with it using his feet, thighs, shoulders and head. Vic and Sean are obviously impressed by his skills. So is Gary, but he is determined not to show it. Calvin ends his performance by nodding the ball to Gary and giving him a challenging look. The game ends with Gary giving an equally impressive display of skills. He turns and gives Calvin a challenging look. Calvin speaks sarcastically.

Calvin Not bad for a white kid.

* *

Outside the City Football Ground on day 8.

Karl Gutke arrives in a taxi. He gets out, pays the driver and approaches the players and officials' entrance where a crowd of TV, radio and newspaper journalists are gathered. Some of them recognise Gutke, and as they crowd round him, microphones are thrust at him, cameras click, and TV camera crews film the scene.

Reporter   Mr Gutke. Can you tell us the latest on the Clark disappearance? Have you any idea what's happened to him?

Gutke   No. I have only just learned about it myself.

Reporter   There's a rumour that he's been kidnapped. Have you anything to say about that?

Gutke pushes through the reporters.

Gutke   No, I have nothing to say ...

Reporter   Have you any idea at all where he could be?

Gutke reaches the door and disappears inside.

* *

Southgate, Gutke and Price are discussing the latest developments. Price is looking out of the window at the crowd of reporters. Southgate is sitting at one end of the long table and Gutke is walking around irritably.

Gutke   But we agreed not to tell the police. You should have told me.

Southgate   Yes. Well ... we didn't have much choice, did we, once they'd got hold of the money? We had to get in touch.

Gutke   But it could put Calvin's life in danger. The kidnappers will be under pressure now. There is no telling what they will do.

Price looks out of the window.

Price   It's like match day out there.

Southgate   Perhaps now that it's public, it'll put the frighteners on them and they'll let him go.

Price	The point is, I couldn't afford to have half a million pounds lying around in a police station. I need every penny I can lay my hands on.
Gutke	Even if it means putting Calvin's life at risk?
	Southgate pauses.
Southgate	Well, if it comes to the worst, at least we're insured.
	Gutke looks at him in disgust.

* *

Inside the derelict flat on day 8.

The atmosphere is tense. Gary and Vic are on edge wondering what to do next.

Gary is sitting on a chair playing with the gun. Vic is standing by the window peering through the boards. Calvin is watching them apprehensively from the sofa and Sean is lying on the mattress reading a comic and listening to the radio on his personal stereo.

Gary swings the gun round the room until he is aiming at Calvin. Calvin pauses.

Calvin	That's dangerous.
Gary	Yeah, I know.
	Sean suddenly sits up.
Sean	They've found out!
Gary	What?
Sean	They know he's missing! It's on the news!
	Gary snatches the headphones off Sean and listens to the news intently. The others watch him. Gary takes off the headphones.
Vic	What did they say?
Gary	Just that he's missing. They didn't say he'd been kidnapped though.

Shooting Stars

Vic I wonder how they found out?
Gary zips up his jacket and walks towards the door.
Where you going?
Gary leaves the flat without answering him.

* *

Inside an interview room at the Police Station on day 8.

Alison is sitting at one side of the table, Detectives Miller and Stone at the other. Stone is writing down Alison's statement.

Alison feels under pressure.

Miller And you say Clark took you straight home? You didn't stop off anywhere?

Alison Of course I am! We drove straight home and he dropped me off outside our house.

Miller What time would that be?

Alison pauses.

Alison I don't know. We left the club about one o'clock. About half past one, I suppose.

Miller And you say there were no witnesses? Did anybody see you?

Alison I don't think so. I wish there were. I wanted the whole street out.

Miller What do you mean?

Alison What's the point in coming home in a Porsche, if there's nobody there to see you?

Stone smiles as he writes this down.

Miller And that was the last you saw of him?

Alison Yeah. He said he was going straight home. He'd go training next morning. I couldn't believe it when I heard. I hope nothing's happened to him.

Miller Right Miss Connor. Thank you very much for your help. If you'll just read your statement and sign it ...

Stone passes the statement across the table.

We'll be in touch if we require further information.

We leave Alison under stress, reading her statement.

* *

Inside an Asian video shop on day 8.

Alison is unpacking a box of new videos on the counter. She is listening anxiously to the news on a transistor radio.

Announcer There is still no news of the missing City footballer Calvin Clark. A police spokesman said they were pursuing several leads but so far they had nothing definite to report. Club officials and the police would make no comment on the rumour that Calvin Clark had been kidnapped by I.R.A. terrorists.

Alison switches off the radio. Gary enters the shop and approaches the counter. Alison is startled to see him. Their conversation is conducted in fierce whispers.

Alison What you doing here?
Gary Was it you who split on us?
Alison Was it heck! What do you take me for?
Gary 'Course it was. You just want him released that's all. You don't care what happens to us.
Alison Do you expect me to care after what you've done?
Gary It was an accident! We didn't mean it!

He hesitates, struggling with his feelings.

It was the thought of you two in the car. I couldn't stand it. I didn't know what I was doing!

Alison realises Gary's anguish and feels for him.

Alison Gary. If you think anything about me you'll let him go. Please! If they find you, you've had it. Just think of your mother. It'll kill her.

Gary pauses.

Gary Will you go out with me if we let him go?

Alison pauses, astonished.

Alison Yeah! Anything! I'll do anything!

Gary pauses.

Gary You must think a lot about him if you'll do that for him.

Alison Do what?

Gary You know. Anything.

Alison I didn't mean that.

Gary What did you mean then?

Alison I didn't mean anything! I just meant I'd do anything to see him free that's all.

Gary speaks angrily.

Gary Yeah, because you're only bothered about him. That's why!

Alison is totally frustrated by him.

Alison Gary! What do you want me to say?

Gary Anyway, we can't let him go now. He'll turn us in. When we get the money I'll be able to disappear.

He pauses.

You can come with me if you like.

Alison is astonished then outraged.

Alison What, with the money you get for Calvin's ransom? What do you take me for?

Gary looks angry and humiliated.

Gary Please yourself. But I'm warning you. If you tell anybody where we are, he'll get it.

He walks away abruptly.

Alison Gary.

But he has left the shop. Alison looks frightened and upset.

* *

Inside the derelict flat at night on day 8.

Gary and Vic are planning their next move. Sean is spraying graffiti.

Vic … Yeah, but it's different now the cops know, isn't it? They'll be all over the place. As soon as you lift the money they'll nick you.

Gary I'll give 'em a warning. I'll tell 'em if they nick me, you'll kill him.

Vic Yeah, but that'll not stop 'em, will it?

Sean puts down his paint can.

Sean I'm starving.

Vic Yeah, and me.

The boys feel in their pockets. They are nearly broke. Gary speaks to Calvin.

Gary You got any money?

Calvin What?

Gary I said, have you got any money? For some food.

Calvin Yeah. In my wallet.

(Sean takes the wallet from Calvin's inside pocket.)

And buy some proper food for a change. I'm sick of snacks.

Sean Do you like Chinese?

Calvin Yeah, anything.

He pauses.

No sweet and sour though. It gives me heartburn.

Sean opens the wallet revealing several twenty pound notes and an array of credit cards.

Sean How much shall I take?

Calvin You're some thief. Asking how much you can take.

Gary Yeah, that's different though, isn't it? Nicking fom somebody's personal. Nicking from shops and that doesn't hurt anybody.

Calvin Take the wallet. Bring me the change.

Gary Go with him Vic. Give him a hand.

Vic Yeah, okay.

Vic leaves the room with Sean.

Sean I'm going to have special fried rice and mushrooms and a crispy pancake roll and …

His voice fades as they walk away. There is an awkward silence between Gary and Calvin. It is the first time they have been alone together since they occupied the flat.

Gary When Alison won the pop quiz, we answered all the questions, me and Vic. Alison knows nowt about it.

Calvin Pity she didn't answer them then.

Gary I saw her today. She says can she have your autograph? She meant to get it when you went out, but she didn't get the chance.

Gary finds a scrap of paper and a biro then suddenly unties Calvin's hands. They face each other. The atmosphere is tense. Is Gary inviting a confrontation? He holds out the pen and paper to Calvin.

Calvin signs his name, then hands it back to Gary. Gary looks at the signature then deliberately tears up the sheet of paper and drops the pieces on the floor.

* *

Inside a Chinese takeaway at night on day 8.

Vic and Sean study the menu board while the owner serves a customer.

Sean What are you having?

Vic Number 24. What about Gary?

Sean He likes 17.

Vic Why don't we have the Chef's Special for four? It looks brilliant.

Sean It's too expensive.

Vic So? We're not buying it.

Sean grins.

Sean Yeah. Okay. We'll pay him back on pay day.

Owner Yes, please?

Sean Chef's Special for six.

Vic For six?

Sean I'm starving.

The owner glances at them suspiciously. They look scruffy. How can they afford such an expensive meal? He calls the order through to the kitchen in Chinese and Vic and Sean sit down on the bench to wait. They glance at the news on the television on the counter, but soon lose interest. Sean takes Calvin's wallet out of his pocket and admires the leather.

Sean It must have cost a bomb.

Vic When we get the money, I'm going down to London to buy some paint. There are shops that sell really good stuff. Stuff you can't get round here.

Sean opens the wallet and examines the contents. The shop owner watches him inspecting Calvin's credit cards, his suspicion growing by the minute.

Sean We could pay by Barclay and keep the money.

Vic Do we look like we've got Barclay cards?

An item on the television news catches their attention.

TV Newsreader ... There has been no further news concerning the disappearance of the English International footballer, Calvin Clark. Rumours that he was in Hamburg have now been discounted. A police spokesman said they are becoming increasingly concerned for the safety of the player and are urging the general public to contact the police if they feel they have any relevant information concerning his whereabouts ...

The owner of the shop notices how avidly Vic and Sean watch this item and how delighted they are at the news. Sean grins.

Sean They haven't got a clue.

The chef brings through the order from the kitchen and the owner packs it into carrier bags.

Owner That will be £22.40p.

Vic And four sets of chopsticks.

Sean pays with two twenty pound notes from the wallet, receives the change, then leaves the shop. Through the window, the shop owner watches them cross the road and go into the flats. He picks up the phone and dials.

* *

Inside the derelict flat at night on day 8.

Gary, Vic, Sean and Calvin are sitting on the floor enjoying their meal. The dishes are spread around between them. Gary, Vic and Sean are all comfortable with their chop sticks. Calvin is less adept and keeps having to use his fingers.

Gary Great ...

Sean speaks to Calvin.

Sean Can you speak German?
Calvin shakes his head.
Calvin No.
Sean What will you do then?
Calvin I'll learn it.
Gary suddenly counts up to ten in German. Calvin looks at him in amazement.
Gary I got GCSE in German.
Vic chips in by counting up to ten in French.
Calvin I suppose you got it in French?
Vic No, my dad was in the Foreign Legion.
They all smile.

* *

Outside the derelict flats at night on day 8.

As Gary is walking towards the flats he notices a movement on a balcony, sees two men on a corner, a car in the shadows … . He glances round. The area is too quiet. There is no one else about. Instinctively, he knows that something is wrong. He carries on walking until he is round the back of the flats then starts to run … Gary is sprinting along the walkway. He reaches the flat and bangs on the door.

Gary Quick! It's the police!

Vic opens the door and Gary rushes in. The boys are in a panic. Calvin tied up on the mattress watches them apprehensively.

Vic Are you sure?
Gary Positive! They're surrounding the place.
Sean I'm going!

Gary unties Calvin's ankles, leaving his wrists bound. He takes out the gun.

Gary Come on! Up!

Vic and Sean look surprised.

Vic What you doing?

Gary He's coming with us.

Vic What for? He'll slow us down. We'll get caught.

Gary He's coming. We're not letting him go now.

Gary pushes Calvin out of the flat. Vic and Sean follow and they run along the walkway to the stairs with Gary prodding Calvin in the back with the gun. They run down the stairs to the next floor. A plain clothes detective spots them from below.

Det. Miller Stop!

They run along the walkway. The lift is standing with its door open at the end of the landing. They pile in, push the button. They are in a state of high nervous excitement. Calvin is terrified. What does Gary intend to do with him? They descend a couple of floors. The doors open. They peer out. All clear. The walkway is deserted. They dash out. The boys know every inch of the flats. They run along walkways, dodging and hiding from the police who spot them at different times, pursue them, communicate through walkie-talkies but cannot catch them. Southgate and Price are standing at the bottom of the flats with a Police Inspector, watching and waiting. Armed plain clothed Police Officers are moving cautiously up the stairs, covering each other at each corner. Calvin, Gary, Vic and Sean are running along a walkway. Gary keeps prodding Calvin in the back with the gun. Vic and Sean bring up the rear. Suddenly, Calvin spins round and lashes out at Gary with his bound hands knocking him to the ground. The gun falls from Gary's hands. Calvin snatches it up and points it at Gary.

Calvin Right, you little bastard! Now what are you going to do?

Vic and Sean freeze. Gary slowly gets to his feet. There is a tense pause then Gary starts to laugh. Calvin is disconcerted by Gary's attitude.

You'll not be laughing when the cops arrive!

Gary Gonna shoot me, are you? There's no bullets in it. Look .... !

Gary takes three bullets out of his pocket and shows them to Calvin, who is momentarily thrown off guard by this revelation. Taking advantage of his indecision, Gary kicks the gun out of his hand and it flies over the balcony rail and drops out of sight. Gary follows up and they engage in a savage fight, falling down and rolling over and over along the walkway.

Vic and Sean look on anxiously. They want to get away. Calvin gets the upper hand. He knocks Gary to the ground, puts the boot in savagely and finishes him off. Gary lies there groaning. Vic and Sean don't know what to do. They want to help Gary but equally they want to escape.

Calvin drags Gary to his feet and holds him by his jacket, staring into his eyes. Then, after a long pause he shoves Gary violently away and he falls to the ground.

Calvin Go on! Piss off!

Gary stares up at him. He can't believe it. Vic and Sean grab him and drag him away before Calvin changes his mind. The three boys run off and disappear down a flight of stairs.

Two armed Police Officers appear at the other end of the walkway. They spot Calvin and run towards him. Calvin slumps against a door and feigns injury as the Officers reach him.

Det. Stone You all right?

Calvin rubs his head and winces.

Calvin Yeah ...

Det. Miller Did you see which way they went?

Calvin pauses.

Calvin I never saw a thing. One of 'em hit me. I went spark out.

Det. Stone Don't worry. We'll get them.

They help Calvin along the walkway.

Calvin emerges from the flats flanked by doctors and police. He appears to be injured. He is limping badly. Gutke looks horrified. What has happened to his star player?

Suddenly Calvin runs at a can and kicks it, then raises his arms as if he has scored a goal. There is nothing wrong with him after all! He was kidding them on! Calvin grins, and with no trace of a limp, walks towards a smiling and relieved Gutke.

* *

Inside the Police Station on day 9.

Gary is standing in an identity parade. The line of young men are roughly the same height, build and colouring. Detective Miller is supervising the line-up.

Calvin Clark enters the room with Detective Stone. Calvin has recovered from his ordeal and looks fit and well.

Det. Stone Right, Mr Clark. Just walk along the line and if you spot him, point him out. Okay?

Calvin nods.

Take your time.

Calvin walks slowly along the line. He reaches Gary and their eyes meet. Calvin displays no reaction. He continues to the end of the line. The two Detectives walk across to him. Calvin shakes his head.

Calvin	He's not there.

Detective Miller looks disappointed.

Det. Miller	Are you sure? Do you want to look at them again?
Calvin	No need. I was with them long enough to know what they look like.

Calvin looks along the line. Gary resists the temptation to turn his head and stares stubbornly ahead.

* *

Outside the City Football stadium day on day 9.

Calvin and Gutke emerge from the players' entrance and walk across the car park towards Gutke's car. Calvin notices Alison standing on her own, waiting.

Calvin	Excuse me for a minute …

Gutke continues towards the car. Calvin walks across to Alison. There is an awkward silence between them. Calvin speaks coolly.

Calvin	Hi. I didn't expect to see you again.

Alison looks embarrassed.

Alison	No. Well …

She doesn't know what else to say. She takes some money out of her bag and hands it to Calvin.

Calvin	What's that for?
Alison	It's the change from the Chinese meal. Sean sent it.

Calvin smiles and shakes his head.

Why did you do it? Let him go, I mean.

Calvin hesitates. He looks away with a troubled expression on his face, then he shakes his head.

Calvin	I don't know.

Alison	Thanks anyway.
	She pauses.
	Can I ask you one last thing?
Calvin	What?
Alison	Can I have your autograph? It's for a friend of mine. She's a big fan of yours.
Calvin	Yeah. Sure.

Alison hands him a notebook and biro.

Calvin signs his name then adds something else. When he hands back the book, Alison is surprised to see that he has written his new address in Hamburg.

That's just in case she wants to write to me.

Alison looks at him in surprise then kisses him on the cheek.

Alison Thanks.

They smile at each other.

Calvin crosses the car park to Gutke's car. Gutke is inside waiting for him. Calvin gets in then waves to Alison as they drive away through the narrow terraced street surrounding the stadium.

The end.

QUESTIONS AND EXPLORATIONS

Two Men from Derby

1 Keeping Track

Here are some questions designed to help you remember the story you've just read.

1   Even though she is pregnant, Freda carries out heavy household jobs without even the offer of any help from the two football scouts. Why?
2   Freda is scared when the two men first arrive – why? Who does she think the men might be?
3   **Freda** *They all say that. They all say that he's a good player ...*
    What do you think Dick might boast of about Freda?
4   Joe Kenny says that centre forwards are '*born not made, like scholars and royalty*'. What does he mean?
5   What do you think stops Dick telling Freda about his football skills?
6   Why doesn't Freda know where Derby is? Find a passage that might explain.
7   Dick isn't often at home. How does he spend his time when he's not working?
8   When George and Joe start describing the first time they saw her husband play, Freda is silent for the first time since they arrived. Why?
9   Why did Dick miss his trial at Sheffield Wednesday? What does Freda think of his excuse?

Questions and Explorations

10 It is clear that Freda wants Dick to go to Derby. Does she think he would be happier?
11 How does Winnie know that Freda wants to talk to her?
12 Mr Turner might really know where Dick is. What would stop his telling Stanley?
13 Dick gives Freda money for housekeeping and '*keeps t'rest for himself*'. What might he spend it on?
14 Why would living in a town appeal to Freda?
15 Why is Freda so quick to point out that she's been married longer than Winnie thought?
16 What does Freda call Winnie's husband, Walter? What does she mean?
17 **Freda** It's easier to think that you could have made it, than know that you didn't.'

What makes her think that this is how Dick feels?

18 Why does Freda take the boots out of the fire? What do you think she will say to Dick about this incident when she sees him? Anything?

2 Explorations

A Characters

1 Choose a character to look at in detail
   a) On a large sheet of paper, draw the outline of a person. Outside the outline, write or draw the pressures and forces that shape the person and inside show the hopes and concerns that make that person who they are.

b) Discuss your diagram with your partner. Does your discussion make you want to change your diagram at all?

2 *'Stuck in here all day washing and ironing and cooking and cleaning. Never going anywhere week in week out.'*

   Is this an accurate description of Freda's life? Write a poem about a typical day in Freda's life. The title might be another line from the play.

3 *'I've always wanted to live in a town.'*

   In groups make a list of all the things that Freda wants. Then discuss:

   – What is she likely to get?
   – What prevents her from getting some things?

4 *'Clever Dick. That's what they used to call him at school. Nobody can tell him owt.'*

   Write two different accounts of Dick at school: a) from the point of view of his class teacher and b) from the point of view of one of the pupils in his class.

5 Choose a cast for the play. Imagine you can use any actor you like – who would you choose?

6 Write notes for the actress playing Freda. What do you expect her to look like? How should she play the role? What use should she make of her voice and her actions?

B Themes

1 One of the main themes of the play (which is set in 1930) is the different lives lived by men and women.

   a) In pairs write down everything that would happen in 'a day in the life of' Freda and then write 'a day in the life of' Dick. How much contact do they have with what the other does?

b) Discuss the lives of men and women today. How much have they changed since 1930, if at all?

2 **a)** The play is set in 1930. When the government wanted women to work for the war effort a few years later, it portrayed them in posters as active and free-thinking; but when the war was over and men needed jobs to return to, women were frequently depicted as beautiful but docile homemakers. See if you can find examples of how men and women are portrayed nowadays.

b) In a group, first, brainstorm words usually associated with women, e.g. gentle, then words associated with men, e.g. independent. Now decide which show either sex in a positive light and which in a negative, to arrive at four categories of words, i.e. women (posative), women (negative), men (positive) and men (negative). Discuss your lists in your groups and try to agree on a joint list.

c) Look again at the play and find examples for each of the four categories. When is a woman shown in a positive or negative light, when a man? Illustrate the moment you have selected by becoming characters with the action frozen to form a still picture. Can the rest of the group guess what point in the play they are seeing? (You can invite them to sculpt the frozen characters to make it clearer still). Ask them to walk around the tableau and describe what they see.

d) Now get the rest of the group to start giving thoughts to the characters they see. How do the thoughts

compare with what the characters are saying?
- **e)** Put yourself in the shoes of the characters in the still picture – would you do or say anything different? Improvise your solution within the context of the scene. Does it improve the situation?

3 Design a poster or leaflet for a performance of the play. Pick out what you think is the most important theme of the play and try to illustrate it in the poster. Also think about the audience you hope to draw in to see the play and make the poster as attractive for them as possible.

C Drama

1 a) Improvise the scene immediately following the end of the play when Dick returns home and Freda tells him that the two men have gone and that he will not get to try out for Derby.

b) Improvise another scene where you have to receive and pass on some bad news.

2 Improvise the scene between Joe and George on the train back to Derby.

3 'Her activity should contrast with the inactivity of the two men who come to visit the house.'

What effects does this stage direction have? Choose a section from the play and perform it with Freda constantly being busy and then with her sitting down and talking to the two men. Which is the most effective and why?

4 *'He never tells me owt. It's his dad who tells me. I go round and do a bit of cleaning up now that his mother's bad.'*

Improvise a scene (perhaps a meal) between these four people in which Freda lets slip about the two men from Derby County.

D Further activities

1. This play contains many stage directions, notes on actions etc. Do you find this helpful?

    Write a scene that has much activity and few words. How do the stage directions contribute to the scene?

2. *Two Men from Derby* was written as a television play. What changes would you need to make if the play was to be presented on stage?

3. **a)** Make a list of all the required furniture and props.

    b) Design a set for the play. Where will the audience be and what are the most important objects? Will it be naturalistic with a working sink and fireplace or will a more abstract set can be used?

4. It might have been useful if the two men from Derby had written to Dick to say they were coming.

    a) Write a letter they might have sent arranging this meeting.

    b) Script the scene where Dick receives the letter. What is Freda's reaction?

5. Imagine that Dick had come home in time, did begin to play for Derby County and scored a goal in an important game. Write a newspaper report about the match.

6. Dick spends a large proportion of his life down the pit and lives for the excitement that football gives him. Write a short story that contrasts these two lifestyles.

GLOSSARY

tackle	equipment
peggy legs	tongs for washing clothes
mangle	machine made of cylinders for pressing the water out of washed clothes
pancheon	baking container
shifts	rotating system of working hours
on her last legs	dying, on the way out
incongruous	out of place
frozen to the marrow	cold through to one's bones
number five shovel	large shovel used in mining
clogging	kicking (with clogs on)
lav	short for lavatory, meaning toilet
the pit	coal mine
bairn	baby
colliers	coal miners
compensate	make up for something
pinny	pinafore or apron
kali	powdered candy
mash	brew tea
Scarlet Pimpernel	red flower but better known as name of successful English spy during French Revolution (1789). George Hirst is referring to the rhyme:
	We seek him here, we seek him there, Those Frenchies seek him everywhere. Is he in heaven? – Is he in hell? That demned, elusive Pimpernel?
	Baroness Orzy (Mrs Montague Barstow) 1865–1947

Shooting Stars

1 Keeping Track

The Stadium – Match Day

1. Why is it Alison who remarks that Calvin isn't married? What is this supposed to tell us about her?
2. Devise a series of questions that you might use to get a profile of one of your mates. How honestly do you think they would answer?
3. *'Tell them it's a routine enquiry and there's nothing to worry about...'* What is Mr Southgate talking about and who is he talking to?
4. Outside the ground, Gary challenges Simmons for chatting up Alison. Look at their conversation and imagine how Alison might react if she could overhear.

After the Match

5. Gary has heard of the two private schools that Mr Groves mentions. What is this meant to suggest?
6. *'Prawns in the game son...'* says the club manager, Price. What has he got wrong? What is it he means?
7. What questions make up the pop quiz? Who has arranged the prize?

The Night Out

8. In the restaurant, everyone treats Calvin like public property. How does he react to all the attention?

9. Alison tells Calvin that her brother sometimes brings champagne home. Think back to the meeting between Groves and Gary in a previous scene. Do you think it's really her brother giving her champagne? If not, why does she say this to Calvin?

10. Gary claims that Calvin is only popular because he is famous. Do you agree?

The Kidnap

11. Think about when the football bosses discuss Calvin's disappearance. In the story it's clear that people have different reasons for wanting him back safe. What are they?

12. What does Sean want to do with his share of the ransom money? What does it tell us about his life?

13. *'It's rich and poor that counts, not black and white...'*
What makes Vic say this and to whom does he say it?

14. Think about when Paula visits Gutke. Why does she bring the newspaper cutting? What is her plan? How does it backfire?

15. Gary was late for the pick-up. How might the story have ended if he had been on time?

16. **Gary** Nicking from someone's personal. Nicking from shops and that doesn't hurt anybody.

    What do you think?

17. In the Chinese takeaway, what clues alert the owner to the identity of the kidnappers?

18. Imagine you are Calvin telling a friend about your ordeal. Why did you let the boys go?

2 Explorations

A Characters

1. Write a player profile for Gary (like the one for Calvin, Alison finds in her football programme). Include your own questions and the answers you think he'd be likely to give. Don't be afraid to include more trivial questions as well as more meaningful ones. What do you think are the main differences between Gary's life and Calvin's?

2. **a)** Draw a silhouette for the characters: Gary, Calvin, Alison, Vic, Sean, Paula and Gutke.

   b) Write what you know about each character inside their outlines. Add to these character notes as you read and re-read the film script.

3. **Alison** 'You must think I'm awful knowing this load of no hopers.'

   How true is this? Find evidence in the film script both for and against Alison's argument.

4. In pairs make a list of objects that are associated with Gary, Calvin, Mr Groves or any of the other major characters in the play.

   What do these objects tell us about the characters? Why is it so unusual for Gary to have a bottle of Chanel No 5 in his pocket?

5. Write a school report or career interview report for Gary. You will need to use your imagination about some of the subjects he has studied as well as evidence from the play.

6. Write Alison's diary entry on the night before going to 'Millionaire's Night Club'. Write one for the day after.

7 a) Early in the film, Mr Groves talks about his need for school uniforms from Riverdale and Bloomfield, two private schools. Write a character profile of a pupils one of these schools.

  b) Compare your character profile with what you know about Gary. Think about the differences between their backgrounds, education, and opportunities.

8 a) In pairs find five positive or good actions that Gary does.

  b) Then discuss: is Gary capable of coping with what life throws at him? Has he failed or has society failed him?

9 In groups discuss: why does Calvin let Gary run off and why doesn't he pick him out in the identity parade?

10 Imagine Gary had been sent to prison and write a letter from him to Alison. What is his writing like? Concentrate not only on what he wants to write but also how he will write it. What is his knowledge of spelling, grammar and punctuation?

B Themes

1 Place a chair in the centre of the room and nominate one person to read out the statements below one at a time. The rest of the group should be free to move around as they like. If you agree with a statement stand as close to the chair as you can. If you disagree put yourself at a distance depending on how much your opinion differs. Don't discuss the results until after the exercise but do make a note of the statements that divide your group.

  a) Women should look nice before a date with a man.

Questions and Explorations

b) Britain is a classless society.

c) You make your own luck.

d) Football stars are overpaid.

e) Black and white people are the same.

f) Only certain people should be allowed to have children.

g) Money can buy anything.

Now try some examples from the play:

h) Nicking from someone's personal. Nicking from shops and that doesn't hurt anybody.

i) It's rich and poor that counts, not black and white.

j) You don't think she likes doing it do you? She's doing it for the money that's all. She's just trying to earn a living. We can't all earn thousands of pounds a week kicking a football around, you know.

k) You've about as much chance of finding a phone around here that works as you have a job.

Finally, get the group back together to discuss your findings. What did people agree about most and what did you disagree about most?

2 What picture is Barry Hines painting of the city in which *Shooting Stars* is set? How realistic do you think the situation is? What evidence can you find from the film to support this?

3 In Gary's life violence is normal. Find the evidence to support this statement. How would you go about changing this?

4 Vic 'So what? What are you trying to say? Just because we're both black don't mean we've got anything in common you know. It's rich and poor that counts, not black and white.'

a) In groups discuss Vic's statement. Do you think he is right?

b) Read what Calvin says before and after Vic's statement. Is Calvin right? Do Calvin and Vic have something in common because Calvin wasn't rich before he became a famous footballer or because they are both black?

C Drama

1. Imagine that you are Gary, Alison, Vic, Sean or Calvin. Can you stand up to a spell in the hot seat? Get other members of the group to ask your character questions and reply as though you were that person. Discuss in the group how it felt to think on that character's behalf.

2. In groups of four, allocate each person a number from 1 to 4. In the following activity number 1 is the most important person and number 4 the least important. Your task is to set out chairs for an important meeting within a short period of time.

    Afterwards, discuss what happened. Who delegated what? Who ended up doing the job? Now think about the three kidnappers. What rank order would you give to them? Do the same for Gutke, Price and Southgate.

3. **a)** Find points in the play where characters are faced with a choice and enact the moments immediately before it, stopping the action at the point a decision needs to be made.

    Act the scene out with two other members of the group playing 'devil' and 'angel' giving opposite advice on each shoulder of the character.

    b) What would happen if the character made a different

decision to the one in the play? Improvise the scene that might follow a different decision.

4 In fours pretend to be tGary's neighbours gossiping about the household. Select some overheard conversations about the family. What does Alison think about the family? What does Alison's mum think?

5 a) Prepare a Radio or TV broadcast about the disappearance of Calvin Clark. You may use interviews with his manager or friends or recordings of Gary's telephone calls.

b) Perform your broadcast. You may also choose to record it.

6 Improvise the police interview between Detectives Miller and Stone and Gary, Vic and Sean.

7 Imagining that Calvin had identified Gary in the penultimate scene of the film, improvise the final scene between Alison and Calvin. Would you want any other characters present?

D Further activities

1 a) What problems and advantages does a film writer have compared to a writer of plays for the theatre?

b) Imagine you are going to direct three scenes from *Shooting Stars* and write director's notes for them.
What settings will you need?
Do these films need to be set on location?
How should the characters be dressed?
What props will you need?
Are you going to use music anywhere and, if so, what and where?

2 Write a preview for *Shooting Stars* for publication in the TV or Radio Times.

3 Calvin signs his autograph a number of times in the film. Identify these moments and think about why each one is different.

Have you ever asked for someone's autograph? Write about your experience and include your reasons and how you felt when you met the person.

4 Write a poem or short story entitled 'Serious Cash Flow Problem'.

GLOSSARY

Rottweiller	German breed of guard dog known to be fierce
whippets	breed of small dogs related to greyhounds
astronomical	enormously large
fluctuating	always changing, rising and falling
the Marquee	popular London venue for rock and pop concerts
Houdini	famous escape artist, died 31 October 1926, aged 52
Dartmoor	high security prison in Devon
reneged	gone back on a promise
D.C.	detention centre (for young offenders)